CROSSING CREEKS,
BRIDGING RIVERS
and LAYING CORNERSTONES

CROSSING CREEKS, BRIDGING RIVERS
and LAYING CORNERSTONES

Recollections of Ronald Crutcher

To my family
My wife Joyce
My children, Susan and Elizabeth
My sons-in-law, Chris Deneen and Baxter Southern
My grandchildren, Andrew, Charlie B., Ellen Anne, Mac,
and Elizabeth

And two women now departed
My grandmother, Marie Crafton Hicks
My mother, Susie Lorene Hicks Woodside

CONTENTS

FOREWORD   vii

PREFACE   ix

ONE—CROSSING CREEKS

Dan German Hospital and Beyond   1
Down on the Farm   7
Monkey Mayhem   13
Pranks, Salesmanship and Tractors   21

TWO—BRIDGING RIVERS

Transitioning to Adulthood   43
The Best and Worst   51
Learning to Adapt in Vietnam   61
Down to Business   85

THREE—KICKING SAND

Real Life   103
Caves, Diamonds and Pigeons   111
Turn East at the Eucalyptus Tree   127

FOUR—LAYING CORNERSTONES

'Back to the Good Ole USA'   165
Excavations, Demolitions and Obsoletion   171
Bringing in a New Perspective   183
Historic Meets Millennial   199
Unexpected Discoveries   207
Considerations—Past, Present and Future   217

Foreword

PROVERBS 11:2 STATES THAT with humility comes wisdom. Having known Ronald Crutcher since the early 1990s, I can attest to what a humble man he is. Throughout my political career in Williamson County, which began in 1986, my association with Ronald in his construction career provided the basis for our business relationship, which has ultimately led to a mutual and admiring friendship.

The 1989 Council on Legislation established "Service Above Self" as the principal motto of The Rotary Club because it best conveys the philosophy of unselfish volunteer service. As a fellow Rotarian, Ronald embodies this motto.

As a volunteer for the Habitat for Humanity of Williamson County since its inception in 1993, Ronald was honored in March 2007, when an entire 26-home subdivision was renamed in his honor to thank him for his work with the non-profit organization. He continues to take personal, subtle pride in his volunteer efforts to help citizens have the opportunity to own their own home.

Synonymous with "humble" one may think of courteous,

kind, and respectful—all of which are valid when one thinks of describing Ronald Crutcher. What you may not—or have not personally witnessed—is the sheepish, mischievous, and lively and bashful young man growing up in Williamson County.

As a Veteran brother, Ron and I have shared some experiences that aren't written within the pages of his book. However, our shared bond for our fellow Veterans is one of humility, integrity, strength, and wisdom. This invisible bond is reflected as you read "between the lines" herein and as you get to know Ron, outside the construction zone, sharing mutual Christian values and a home-cooked meal and a freshly baked pie.

Rogers C. Anderson, USAF (1968-1971)
Williamson County Mayor
November 2020

PREFACE

THIS BOOK CAME ABOUT as a result of two separate events. I was given a pamphlet written by David Wood, one of my former Battle Ground Academy ‘BGA’ teachers, and later, mentor at Vanderbilt. While discussing it he said that he had written it for his family, and I should write some of my history for mine.

About the same time one of my grandsons, Mac, came to me and wanted to hear about my daddy, uncles and cousin winning the Silver Give-Away at the Sulphur Dell ballpark. I repeated the tale and saw his interest by the undivided attention he was giving.

As I began writing my story my wife Joyce encouraged me to record more than I had anticipated. She reminded me that my time spent in Vietnam and Saudi Arabia were unique experiences and that others may also want to read about my life.

Since we were spending a lot of time at home together during the coronavirus pandemic of 2020, we had a lot of time for me to write and for her to edit. Also, with the help of Pam Horne and Caroline Harwood, I was able to produce a book that I hope will be enjoyed by my family as well as those who enjoy reading about others.

CROSSING CREEKS

1
Dan German Hospital and Beyond
1945 – 1951

FRANKLIN, TENNESSEE IN 1945 was quite different than it is today. One could find an auto dealer, a bank, grocery, drugstore, five-and-dime, hardware, and dry goods store on Main Street. There were two hospitals just off Main. On June 10 of that year, I was born in one of them—Dan German.

My mother, Susie Lorene Hicks, had married Roy E. Crutcher in 1944. She was only fifteen when I was born. Roy Crutcher's name is on my birth certificate; however, they divorced in 1945. He was later killed in a construction accident in 1953 while on a job with the Tennessee Department of Transportation. After Mother's divorce the two of us lived with my grandparents, Mama and Daddy Hicks, on a farm that we always called "the Spratt Place". It was situated on the Duplex-Spring Hill Road in the south-central part of Williamson County. My first memories of life begin there.

Daddy Hicks ate hot green peppers. I got my hands on one, ate it, and immediately started crying because it was so hot. I made it worse when I rubbed the tears and got the pepper on

1

my face. With the help of butter, I survived. I still like hot peppers.

Mother married Everett Blythe Woodside on March 21, 1947. I consider him as my daddy. We lived on the John Lee, Sr., farm where Daddy worked as a day laborer. My brother, Everett Ray Woodside, was born July 11, 1948. This also happened to be Daddy Hicks' birthday.

By the end of that same year, we had moved to Owl Hollow Road, which was about two miles north of the Lee Farm. Owl Hollow ran from Highway 431 'Lewisburg Pike' to Duplex-Spring Hill Road, today called Duplex Road, just outside Spring Hill. Daddy made a trade 'contract by handshake' to farm the land for a portion of the crops and rent-free housing for our family. All the farming was done with mules and draft horses, no tractors.

Our closest neighbor was an African American family whose last name was Beech. They had a truck garden where they raised vegetables to sell in Franklin. They took me with them one Saturday. The trip started with me eating breakfast at their house before daylight; it was the first and last time I ate turnip greens for breakfast.

We made stops at several places before heading home. Our last stop was at Henry's Market at 301 Lewisburg Avenue. This was where I saw my first train, and I was fascinated by it. I was four years old at the time.

My little brother Ray learned to walk while we lived at Owl Hollow. One morning while he was still crawling, he got too close to the wood-burning cook stove and hit the stick Mother used to hold the broken oven door closed causing it to open. The hot door burned his wrist so severely that the skin came off.

He had the scar his entire life.

The women folk would visit in the afternoons during summer, just between dinner 'lunch' and supper 'dinner'. One afternoon a lady came over with her children. While the ladies talked 'gossiped' on the porch we young'uns 'children' played in the creek in front of the house. There was a bridge over the creek where a family of skunks lived in the stone abutments. We had watched the skunks come out and play many times. In fact, Daddy had picked up the little skunks once, before their scent glands were developed, and let Ray and me hold them. So, on this summer afternoon, show-off Ronald caught one of the little skunks to show our guests. It covered me with spray! It had grown up.

Mother would not let me back in the yard. Instead, she marched me to the water trough, stripped my clothes, scrubbed me until my skin was raw with lye soap, and had me put on clean clothes. This was in front of the neighbor's kids. I lost a good pair of overalls and dignity in that ordeal.

Our mailbox was at the end of a long gravel road; we didn't call them driveways. Ray and I would walk to the mailbox at Owl Hollow Road. One day Ray wanted to carry the mail to the house. I wouldn't let him. Remember, I was five and he only two. Ray got so mad he picked up a large flat rock and threw it at me. It mashed my big toe causing blood to go everywhere. I dropped to the ground and screamed for him to go get Mother and the Germtrol. Mother heard us hollering and came running. She brought rags for a bandage and the bottle of Germtrol. Incidentally, Germtrol was sold as a disinfectant by a traveling salesman we called the Watkins' Man. He made regular stops at homes out in the country. My wound healed, but after that Mother gave strict orders for us to share the carrying of the mail.

Ray and I were "kidnapped" while we were living in Owl

Hollow. Two young women appeared one afternoon and said that they had met our Uncle Raymond, Daddy's brother, in New York. Raymond was in the Army, stationed outside New York City. The ladies said he had invited them to stop by his family's place if they were ever in the area. Mother and Daddy invited them to stay overnight. The next day they asked Daddy if they could ride the work horses. He said, "It's okay, but I have no saddles."

Later in the day, they got on the horses and took Ray and me with them, leaving the farm without telling Mother or Daddy. We then proceeded to the general store about three miles away. When Mother awoke from her afternoon nap, she discovered that we were gone and screamed for Daddy. He immediately started running across the fields and through the woods to the store. He got there just as the women were buying us soft drinks. He took Ray and me by the hand and ordered them to immediately return to the house.

Meanwhile, back at the house, Mother went through their luggage and found a pistol. When they returned with us, they were told to catch a ride on the flatbed truck our neighbor was taking into town that night. Ray and I got a cold drink and candy out of this adventure. The last we saw of these women was them sitting with their baggage on the back of Uncle Sam's truck, along with six or seven African Americans, who were making their usual Saturday trip to the general store in Spring Hill where there was a Greyhound bus stop.

Daddy's youngest sister Gladys came to live with us so she could finish the eighth grade. She had dropped out of school, but the State of Tennessee had required her to go back because she was not sixteen years old. Occasionally, she would take me with her to nearby Mt. Carmel Elementary. It had eight grades in one room with another room used for the kitchen. The toilets were outside in two outhouses, one for boys and one for girls. Mother and Daddy wanted better for me. More about that later.

2
DOWN ON THE FARM
1951 – 1954

WE MOVED ON THANKSGIVING day in 1950 to my great grandmother Crafton's farm nearby, which was next to the Lee Farm on Lee Lane. Mrs. Crafton was Mama Hicks' mother. Daddy had made a trade with her to farm as a share tenant farmer. Her husband, Jim Crafton, had died; she decided to move to Old Hickory, Tennessee to live with her daughter, who we called Aunt Jimmie.

Thanksgiving Day was so hot that everyone worked in their T-shirts. Without warning the weather turned sharply cold, so much that it snowed that night. The next morning, Daddy hurriedly hooked up the wood-burning stove, but there was no wood ready to burn. He found the axe covered in snow and then was able to split some logs for a fire. Winter had set in. In January a blizzard hit with snow and ice. We were isolated; the ice had broken tree limbs blocking the roads. Since we didn't have a car, it was no big deal.

The house where we lived was inhabited by ghosts. For years they could be heard walking in the attic late at night. Everyone was afraid to go into the attic after dark. After we moved in, we heard the ghosts. Daddy, along with a cousin who worked on the farm, and one of my uncles were all three bound and determined to solve the mystery of the ghosts. One night one of the men went into the attic and waited. When he heard the ghosts, he tapped on the ceiling. Another person stood by the attic light switch and, after hearing the tapping, flipped on the switch. Lo and behold, the mystery was solved! The ghosts were flying squirrels, a family of them—caught stealing walnuts drying in the attic. They probably had been raised in a nest nearby for generations and inherited the cache of walnuts.

Ray avoided another close call while we were playing, this time in the pond in front of our house. We were playing in the mud in early spring, just two and five years old at the time. Somehow, Ray fell in the water and got too far from the bank for me to pull him out. I ran to the house and got Mother. She ran into the water, rescuing Ray. He coughed up muddy water. The pond was off limits from that point on.

While living in Owl Hollow, Daddy found an orphaned baby goat and brought him home. Mother raised the goat on a baby bottle; we named him Billy. He moved with us to the Crafton Place and became very mean as he got older. When Ray would go outside into the yard, Billy would butt him. Finally, Daddy had had enough. He made a deal with our African American neighbors to kill, dress, and butcher Billy. I was the only one who could handle Billy; so, I was sent to get him from the field where he was grazing with the cows. I led him back by his horns to the slaughter, crying with each step. Curiosity overcame my sorrow; I watched Daddy every step of the process. Mother cooked Billy, crying each time she opened the pot. All of us were sad, but that goat was good! I still like goat or lamb.

In 1951, I turned six. Time to go to school! I was due to go to Mt. Carmel Elementary–one room, one teacher, eight grades. To avoid this, I was sent to live with my grandparents and Uncle Floyd, who was several years older than me. They lived further north in the county on Mallory Station Road. Floyd and I were to attend Lipscomb Elementary School on Concord Road. As we say now, "It was state-of-the-art." It was new and had eight classrooms, eight teachers, a cafeteria, and indoor toilets that flushed. (Coincidently, forty years later I was a partner in the company that demolished this school and built a new one.) Floyd and I rode the school bus to Lipscomb until he was older and bought a Model T Ford pickup truck (think Jed Clampett's character in *The Beverly Hillbillies*).

My first-grade teacher was Mrs. Stanley. She was good and ran a tight ship. I got into so much trouble talking during class that it seemed like I stood in the corner daily. Each morning I hung my coat on the corner coat hook so I could stand behind it and sleep. If you were really bad, she took you in the toilet room and banged on the commode, making the other kids think you were getting a spanking. I never made it to the toilet room.

One weekend, when I was home with my family, I had a serious accident (all my making). Ray and I had watched the portable feed grinder come to the farm and grind the corn for livestock feed. We were fascinated by the power and noise! The next day, I got the bright idea that Ray and I could have our own feed grinder. I took the reel lawn mower and turned it upside down. I made Ray pull it while I stuck corn shucks in the spinning reel. In less than three minutes, I stuck my left little finger in with the shucks. Only a small strip of skin kept it from falling off. I was carried to Franklin to see Dr. Adolphus Bray so he could sew my finger back on. The next day at school I was the center of attention with a splint, bandages, and a tale to tell.

I went back to Dr. Bray in two weeks. When the bandages were removed, the black color of my finger told everyone that the surgery was not successful. I was put in the hospital for removal of the finger. The surgery was a piece of cake. The recovery of a day or two was fantastic—all the time sherbet and ginger ale I wanted, anytime. I had never had either before, so I hated to leave the hospital. Back to school for another show-and-tell. I loved every minute of it!

I had only one serious episode outside the classroom. One afternoon while I was waiting for the school bus a much older cousin started picking on me. I picked up a large rock and cold-cocked him just above the left eye. It was a good shot and drew a lot of blood. The next morning the principal was waiting for me at the front door. He asked what happened and I told him. Uncle Floyd verified my explanation. The matter was closed; I was no longer bothered by the older boys.

I met my life-long friend David Moran at Lipscomb Elementary. We remain friends to this day. We went to school together, were in the Boy Scouts together, and graduated from Vanderbilt on the same day.

The summer before I entered second grade, Mama and Daddy Hicks, Uncle Floyd, and I moved to the Spring Hill area. Uncle Floyd had made a trade to work on Mr. Mitchem's farm, which meant that I would ride the school bus to Thompson

Station Elementary School. It was a modern school building like Lipscomb.

My teacher at the first of the year was Mrs. Bethurum from Franklin. She would bring books from the public library in Franklin for us to read. The library at our school was not very extensive. I read most of the books before she had to return them. I particularly liked the hardcover biographies of the explorers. I could always spot them among the stack of books because the covers were a dark shade of orange. My imagination would get me lost with Lewis and Clark as they explored the untamed Missouri Territory.

After a few weeks, Mrs. Bethurum asked for volunteers to go to the first-grade room with Mrs. Taft. As I had a habit of doing then, and still now, I stuck my hand up not knowing the details of what I was getting into. The purpose of moving six students was to balance class sizes. I had learned a lot in first grade at Lipscomb, so I helped Mrs. Taft teach the new first graders to read and worked with them on arithmetic.

I must have been rambunctious, because during the afternoons at nap time Mrs. Taft would let me sleep after she woke the other students. Sometimes she had to wake me to catch the school bus.

Marble playing went on during recess, lunch break, and after school. We had a game that involved throwing your marble to hit the other player's marble. One of the boys' father drove a bulldozer. The boy showed up at school on a Monday with a steel ball bearing about the size of a large marble. There was no rule book for our game, but his steel ball bearing interrupted our daily competition. In fact, he stopped us from playing by breaking our glass marbles.

The marble game kept us entertained; it could also easily cause distraction. One afternoon after school, I was playing marbles and missed my school bus. I knew the bus route, so I ran down Columbia Pike about a mile to Buckner Road, getting there just as the bus came to a stop on Columbia Pike. I got on and rode the rest of the way home.

Most days, I caught and got off the school bus at the farm next door and walked through the fields to our house. This was less than a mile and required crossing a small creek. Several times, Daddy Hicks would come looking for me and find me wet and muddy from playing in the creek. I was often playing a game where I would jump across the creek, narrow part first, then wider, wider, and wider until the creek was so wide that I fell in.

Uncle Snooks and Aunt Allie Mae lived on the farm next to us. He milked the cows on the place where we lived. One afternoon he sent me to drive a cow with her newborn calf to the barn. The cow had other ideas. She butted me down to the ground with her head and horns. My uncle heard me screaming and came running with a stick to stop the cow. I was scared, but okay.

Uncle Snooks and Aunt Allie Mae had a rat problem in their house. Uncle Snooks sat up one night in the dark with the lights off, his 12-gauge shotgun in his lap. There was a flashlight taped to the gun. When he heard the rat running across the floor, he cut the flashlight on and fired. He killed the rat but blew a hole in the door behind the rat. Blood and rat guts went everywhere. Uncle Snooks always had a different approach to problems. The minister at his funeral called his escapades "Snookums."

3

MONKEY MAYHEM
1954 – 1959

ONE NIGHT IN THE mid-1950s, the menfolk went to Sulphur Dell Baseball Stadium to see the Nashville Vols baseball team play. The big promotion that night was the Silver Give-Away. During the seventh inning break a wheelbarrow of silver coins (real silver back then) was rolled to the pitcher's mound. A ticket stub was drawn. When the lucky fan came to the field, he was given a scoop to use to pour as many coins into a burlap bag as he thought he could carry from the pitcher's mound to home plate. If he could carry the bag, he got to keep the money. If he dropped the bag, he lost it.

The group of menfolk who went that night included my dad, Uncle Snooks, Uncle Tom, Cousin Robert Waddey, and Uncle Floyd. Robert was the strongest. They agreed that if anyone's ticket stub was drawn, they would pass it to Robert. They also agreed to split the money in six equal portions with each

13

getting a share, and the one remaining share would go to the actual stub owner.

Robert's stub was drawn. He walked to the pitcher's mound, scooped coins in the bag, and tested the weight several times. When he had what he thought he could carry, he walked straight to home plate and set the bag down. He won the jackpot!

After the money was counted, my dad and the group learned they had won exactly $999.50. A newspaper reporter asked Robert why he hadn't put in two more quarters to make an even $1,000. He replied, "That may have been more than I could carry." This was the record amount ever won on Silver Give-Away night.

Daddy made a trade in 1953 with Tom Robinson to move to his farm on Riverside Road. The farm was in Williamson County's Twelfth Civil District, which, back then, included the city of Franklin. Franklin had its own school district with nice buildings and good teachers, but no school buses. Mr. Scales, the county school superintendent, allowed Ray and me to ride the county's bus to Franklin High School. (There was just one high school back then.) We caught the bus about a mile from our house. We were dropped off at the high school, which was three blocks south of the Franklin Elementary School at Five Points. Ray was in the first grade; I was in the fourth. We attended that city school through the fifth grade before going to the new Franklin Junior High School on Academy Street.

We were warned not to throw rocks at each other because an eye could be blinded. However, one afternoon on our mile walk home from the bus, Ray and I started throwing rocks. One of mine caught Ray in the eye; he screamed and covered it with his hand. "I can't see! You will have to lead me home," was his demand. I did lead him as he continued to scream and cry. This went on for about a half mile.

Mother heard Ray when we neared the house and came running to us, screaming out the words, "What happened?" By that time, I was crying as I told her that I had hit Ray's eye with a rock and put it out. She told us that we had to go get Daddy from the field so we could carry Ray to the doctor. Ray suddenly started laughing, took his hand from his eye, and blurted out.

"I was only kidding!" he confessed.

I was ready to hit him with my fist—not a rock. We didn't throw any more rocks.

There were a couple of incidents at Franklin Elementary that I remember. During recess we boys (the girls were separated from the boys by a sidewalk) played a game we called "Kill the Man with the Ball." A football was tossed up, and the one who caught it was mobbed by the rest of us. One of my rich classmates showed up one Monday with a nice, shiny football helmet that he had gotten at a Vanderbilt football game the Saturday before. He was very protective and proud of his helmet. The first time he got the ball someone grabbed the face guard and almost took his head off. That was the last time we saw the helmet.

Another incident occurred in fifth grade. My teacher was Mrs. Josephine Wirt. We had room mothers, who would have a party for us once a month that included some sort of game or program and treats. One month our room mother, Mrs. McKeand, asked her friend, Mrs. Rice, to bring the pet monkey that stayed in the Rice's yard on Lewisburg Avenue. Mrs. Rice had it

15

secured on a leash when she brought it into the classroom. But the noise we students made upset the monkey, and he slipped out of the leash.

The loose monkey attempted to make one trip around the room, starting on the picture rail that hung above the chalkboards, before he dropped down onto Mrs. McKeand's shoulders, and, with both his hands, grabbed a handful of her hair. Then, Mrs. McKeand made a couple of trips around the room. We were screaming and laughing so much that the principal came to see what was happening. He stopped Mrs. McKeand long enough to take the monkey off her. The monkey was expelled from school, never to return. It died years later of old age at the Rice's home on Lewisburg Avenue.

———————⌇———————

Mrs. Wirt was one of the major blessings of my life. She saw something in me, took me under her wing, and used all of her friends to help me. She got Dr. Beasley to fix my terrible teeth, and she gave me a job in the classroom taking care of the guppy fish. The job paid enough for me to pay my dues to a fund set up by the room mothers that paid for the goodies for the monthly party. This was a good job, except for the weekend the thermostat on the heater quit working and the fish got cooked. Cleaning out the mess on Monday was no fun.

Mrs. Wirt and my mother wore the same dress size. She would give Mother her slightly used clothes and shoes. We, in turn, kept the Wirts in fresh vegetables in season. Mrs. Wirt's husband, Winard, worked for a large printing company in Nashville. They couldn't have children, but raised a niece, who became a nurse. She took care of Mrs. Wirt in her final years.

The best thing Mrs. Wirt did for me was to tell me that I

should be in Johnny Green's Boy Scout Troop #153. This was when I was in the sixth grade. Johnny caused me to make my first major decision. He told me I could be in the Scouts or in the 4-H Club. But he said I couldn't succeed in both. I chose the Scouts. My friend David Moran joined also. David and I were in Boy Scouts until we went to Vanderbilt.

Scouting taught me as much as my school classes. I earned twenty-one merit badges to get my Eagle Award. The experiences involved in earning each badge taught me skills that I would later need. For example, map reading was a key part of the Orienteering Badge. The content was so thorough I needed nothing more to get me through my Army training years later.

The merit badges taught me a lot about myself. I did not know how to swim when I joined the Scouts. It took two summer camps to learn to swim. Three years later, I was trying to earn the lifesaving merit badge, a requirement for the Eagle Award, when I almost failed the test.

Our task was to pull a grown man (a Scout counselor) from Old Hickory Lake. I drew the roughest counselor. When I swam out to save him, he was kicking and fighting exactly like a drowning person. When I got too close to him, he grabbed me, pushed me under the water, and placed his foot on my submerged shoulder. He pushed me so deep that I was in a pocket of ice-cold water. I got loose from him and surfaced several feet from him. Spitting lake water, I swam to the dock and left the counselor to drown, knowing I had failed the test and would not get my Eagle.

The next Scout to try to rescue the drowning man was a boy who had lost his left hand above the wrist. He swam to the man, did a perfect save, and brought the man back to the dock. At that point I said to myself, "If a boy with one hand can do that, so can I." I then asked for a second chance and got it. This time I was faced with a different drowning victim. I succeeded in the rescue. This episode taught me not to give up but to always try again after you fail.

17

Johnny Green taught us map reading using United States Geological Survey topography maps, the same topo maps used in the Army. During my officer's basic training at Fort Belvoir, Virginia in the winter of 1968, I was in an exercise in which we were taught map reading. Because we were considered 'green' by Army standards, we were skill tested by being dropped off far from base in the cold, cold night and directed to find our way back to the camp. We were about four miles from camp. Situated between us and the camp, there was a lake that had a thin sheet of ice on its surface.

With our topo map, compass, flashlight, and a poncho to cover the light, we attempted to read the map. Meanwhile, a unit of regular soldiers was positioned between us and the camp. The soldiers were instructed to apprehend us as prisoners of war. I had two lieutenants with me, one from New York and one from Connecticut. Once dropped off, we were left to our own devices to find our way back to camp. My companions wanted to huddle alongside the road, but I took charge and moved us deep into the woods before we could be caught.

After walking about a hundred yards we stopped to plan our route. The other two wanted to take compass bearings and pace off how far we had walked. I told them that this was no more than a "possum hunt," and that the map indicated we were on a ridge that would lead us to a small stream. The stream, I said, would lead to the lake we had to get around. They wanted to know how I knew this. My reply was, "I learned map reading in Boy Scouts."

They were skeptical and asked how far it was to the stream. I told them a hundred yards; I was guessing. We headed in the right direction, counting our steps. As luck would have it, we reached the stream when our step count measured a hundred yards. For the remainder of the night they did everything I told them and did not complain. We had heard that the regular soldiers would be picked up at midnight. Fortunately, we saw a group of them before they saw us; so, we lay in the bushes until midnight. Sure enough, the Army truck came by, picked them up, and left. We hit the road to our camp. We were one of the first groups back; we got a good night's sleep in the warm barracks.

Interstate 65 was built through Mr. Robinson's farm in 1958. To get from one side of the farm to the other, we had to use a road that was built under the interstate bridge at the Harpeth River. This road was a part of the construction project. The building of I-65 was fascinating to my family, but particularly to Daddy and me. A large chunk made up of rock and mud was thrown through the roof of Mr. Robinson's barn when the contractor, Brindley Brothers, was dynamiting. The contractor hired us to repair the hole in Mr. Robinson's roof. We were paid the wage scale dictated by the federal government. Daddy was hired as a carpenter; I was a laborer. We made more for two hours work than we could make in a ten-hour day on the farm.

Daddy became friends with Brindley's superintendent, who, from the beginning of the job, drove a new Ford car every day to the worksite. As the job was nearly finished, a boulder had to be blasted from a bluff beside the road. First, the huge rock was drilled, and the dynamite loaded. Next, one of the crew drove the superintendent's car onto the boulder, parked it, and got out. Daddy saw what was happening and went running to the superintendent just as the rock and car exploded. He then realized that this was done on purpose so the superintendent could get a new car for the next job. The building of I-65 probably started my interest in construction.

4

PRANKS, SALESMANSHIP AND TRACTORS
1959 – 1963

I WENT TO BATTLE GROUND Academy from the fall of 1959 until I graduated in the spring of 1963. BGA is a private school that was founded in Franklin in 1889. The school was coed until 1929, at which time it became all male. At the time I attended, the campus accommodated boarding students, as well as day students like me. The pranks that were pulled were hilarious! I did my share beginning freshman year.

We had an English teacher who was new at BGA. He was determined that we were to study everything that was printed in the textbook, including what we considered to be "junk" in the front of the book. One of the "junk" chapters was on salesmanship, another on public speaking. Our classroom assignment was to model a sales call using our preferred product. We picked our item to sell, went outside the classroom, knocked on the door, walked in and introduced ourselves to the teacher, **Mr.**

Bob Knight, and sold our product.

I had seen a business card nailed to a telephone pole that was advertising Superior Paper Matches. The business's salesman was a local character named Freddie Buford; he had a speech impediment. Everyone in the class knew Freddie, except Mr. Knight, who was new in Franklin. When it was my turn, I went outside the room, knocked on the door and was invited in. I said, "Halloo, my nam' is Freddie Bufoor,' and I am gonin' to sell you some matches." The room broke out in laughter. Mr. Knight slapped a book on the desk several times before my classmates stopped laughing. He gave the loudest boys three demerits for being disrespectful to me.

Now I had a problem. I hadn't thought beyond my introduction. Mr. Knight (we later nicknamed him Bub Nutt) asked me the name of my company, what could be printed on the match covers, and the cost. I replied, "Superior Matches, five dollars for a box of a dozen, or fifty dollars for a gross." I got a B for my presentation and learned what an impromptu speech was.

Bub Nutt never got us under control. The headmaster switched teachers with the junior class at semester break. We got Mr. Naylor, and the juniors got Bub Nutt.

Mr. Naylor (nicknamed Goober because he was always eating peanuts) had a habit of coming into the classroom, going to the window, raising it and spitting. After shutting it, he started class. One day Bubby Beasley got the bright idea of raising the window before class. Then, Mr. Naylor came in and proceeded straight to the window. He immediately lowered the window, spit on it, raised it back, and then held class. In addition to teaching, he oversaw production of the BGA annual, *The Cannonball*. A tradition was to hear him make this announcement in assembly: "Anyone with darkroom experience is needed on the annual staff." It always drew laughter.

22

If the boarding students were not on the honor roll, they had to attend night study hall in the auditorium. One night when Mr. Naylor was keeping study hall, the students gathered their alarm clocks and divided them into three groups. Each group had their alarms set to go off fifteen minutes apart. They were hidden on outside window ledges, in desks, and above the tile ceiling. When the alarms started going off, Mr. Naylor started running from one ringing clock to another. By the time he got the first group silenced, another would start. This went on for forty-five minutes. There was little studying and much laughter that night.

Our report cards were sent home by the students. I got one bad card. BGA Headmaster, Mr. Redick ('we called him Bun'), wrote, "Ronald's attitude could improve." Mother and Daddy wanted an explanation. This was my junior year. One of my classes was typing, taught by Mrs. Redick, Bun's wife. One day in class, she described something by calling it "a smidgen of ...."

My best friend David Moran then asked her, "What is a smidgen?" Smart-mouth me popped up and interjected, "David, don't you know a smidgen is a smit more than a smat?" Mrs. Redick gave me a verbal dressing down but no demerits. She must have told her husband. Daddy told me that was the last time he wanted to see comments like that from Mr. Redick on my card. It was.

One of Mr. Naylor's required duties was to be in charge of the concession stand during football season. He met the Coca Cola truck, ordered the drinks, and had the stand cleaned at the beginning of the season. He supervised the students hired to run the stand and collected the money after each game.

David and I were hired to work the stand our first year at BGA. By our sophomore year, Mr. Naylor had passed all his duties to us. At the beginning of our junior year, we asked if candy bars could also be sold since the fans wanted to buy them. Mr. Naylor told us that was too much trouble. We then asked if we could sell them. He said it would be okay if we bought the candy ourselves and kept the money separate. We then went to Walgreens in Green Hills, where we could find the cheapest price. We bought the candy bars for 10¢, then sold them for 25¢.

At the beginning of the next football season, Mr. J.B. Akin, BGA's business manager, asked us what we were getting for running the concessions. We said, "You are paying us $15 a night and we make about $20 off the candy sales." He was shocked that we made so much from the candy. Mr. Akin allowed us to continue, but he added that when we graduated the proceeds from the candy bar sales would go to the school thereafter.

Mr. J.B. Akin was a good, fair man who looked out for students, particularly me. He had to save every penny to keep BGA financially sound. One summer he was having a new vinyl tile floor installed in the assembly hall. Rather than pay the contractor to remove the desks that were screwed to the old floor, he hired me. There were about 150 desks with eight screws per desk, totaling 1200 screws. He gave me a manual Yankee screwdriver and a bucket for the removed screws, then left me alone. I rode my bicycle with a brown-bagged lunch from my house on Mr. Robinson's farm to BGA, a distance of about five miles. I think it took a couple of weeks to complete the job. I appreciated the money and BGA appreciated not having to pay carpenter's wages.

Mr. Akin and his wife Katherine would often take the boarding students on an outing. One Saturday night they carried a group to the Hippodrome in Nashville to watch live wrestling, which some people said was fake. The Akins sat high above the wrestling ring on the back row. During the event a fight broke out among the fans. Mr. Akin recalled later that he was laughing until the moment he saw the BGA boys in the middle of the melee. But he reacted quickly. He managed his way through the crowd with Katherine, signaled the boys it was time to go, and herded the group to the bus so everyone could immediately head back to Franklin. It was some time before there was another wrestling trip.

BGA was a football powerhouse in the early sixties. Even though the school had less than 250 high school students, the team held the title of Butter Bowl Champs in 1959. They were the winners of the 1960 Clinic Bowl by defeating Isaac Litton High School. This game was recognized as the TSSAA State Championship.

Other schools wanted to know how BGA pulled it off since no athletic scholarships were allowed by Tennessee Secondary School Athletic Association. The answer was simple. Every boy was convinced they could play football, yours truly included.

I went out for the football B Team at the urging of the coach, Mr. Smithson (nicknamed Goat). I probably weighed 120 lbs. dripping wet. My friend David had grown into a body of probably 160 or 170 lbs. On the first full day of practice we had a drill where we ran at each other and tried to knock each other down. I drew David, thinking to myself that he would be easy on me. Wrong! He hit me with every pound he had on his body. I don't know whether his lick or the ground knocked me out, but one did. I quickly recovered and kept on practicing.

I was sub to the subs. When Coach Smithson was ready to pull a player out of the game, he sent me in. In one game he substituted me for the tackle for one play. The other team saw me coming! I counted eleven sets of cleats going over my face.

My knuckle was split in practice and taped by Goat. He told me that I didn't need to go to the doctor. After two weeks it was not healing; so, I saw a doctor. When he looked at my x-rays, he could see the break, but he said it had been too long to do anything except put a cast on it. That ended my football career. I decided track was my sport.

In the spring I went out for track. I had no track shoes, but another classmate gave me a pair of new shoes that were too small for him. I was a distance runner. I lettered and won one race, not a spectacular career but enjoyable.

Mr. Akin would hire David and me during the summer to work around the school. Part of our job was to move stuff using the school's small Farm All tractor and low trailer. Having been hired first, I had seniority, meaning I got to drive the tractor. One day we were going around the track with me driving the tractor and David standing on the trailer. I happened to look back just as David jumped from the trailer, hit the track on his feet, and then rolled forward almost as fast as the tractor was going. By the time I got the tractor stopped, so had David.

"What were you doing?" I asked him.

David's reply was, "trying to defy Newton's Law of Motion."

I knew it well. 'An object at rest stays at rest and an object in motion remains in motion with the same speed and the same direction unless acted upon by an unbalanced force.' David was the object and the track was the unbalanced force. Mr. Oxley, our physics teacher, would have been proud of David if he had known about the experiment even though it failed.

Mr. Akin asked David and me if we knew where his wife Katherine could get some ferns for her flower garden. David said that there were none at his place on the Moran Farm. I told Mr. Akin that there were some in the woods where we camped

26

as Boy Scouts. I offered to take him there and help him dig some for transplanting. He took me up on my offer. We went during a study hall and got a few ferns. At graduation I received the Bob Carter School Spirit Award. Mr. Akin was the faculty member who selected the award winner.

David and I didn't limit all our endeavors to BGA. One spring I got the bright idea to build a flat-bottom boat to float on the Harpeth River behind our house. We took some scrap lumber and some tar from a nearby gas line that was being laid and some burlap to caulk the joints. We built it on flat rocks near the river. After measuring ourselves lying down, since we wanted to sleep in it, we began the process with hand saws, hammer and nails, and tar melted in a bucket over a wood fire. The only mishaps occurred when I burned my hands and arms several times trying to put out the fire when it jumped into the tar bucket. The burns were second degree. I literally put some skin in the boat project.

After three or four weekends of work, it was ready to launch. Due to its size, thick lumber, and the amount of tar, it was so heavy that it took three men plus David and me to get it to the river. Into the Harpeth River it went with a splash! We spent an hour or so floating on the river using poles we had cut to guide it. It was definitely a two-man boat! It took one of us to push it with the pole and the other to bail out the water that leaked into it. We turned it over on a sand bar and planned to fix the leaks with more tar the next weekend.

That night a heavy rainstorm came and raised the water in the river over the sand bar. We hadn't thought to tie the boat to a tree because it was so heavy. The next morning, I went to check on the boat. No boat! That afternoon after school, I searched the river for a mile but I had no luck.

Several years later, it appeared upside down in the Harpeth

almost to Franklin, about four miles by river from where we launched it. It was across the river from Lewisburg Pike lodged in heavy timber trash. I left it, and watched it for several years. After that, I restored an old fishing boat and an Old Town canoe with more success.

David and I were elected to the Order of the Arrow, an honorary society in the Boy Scouts of America. There are three levels of membership: Ordeal, Brotherhood, and Vigil. The first level was all book work. The second, Brotherhood, was tough. We had to spend twenty-four hours in silence with minimum food and water. We did this at Camp Boxwell. In daylight hours we worked silently, clearing brush and trees for future campsites on the property. I made it through okay until that night.

A group of us were led through the camp's dark woods to go to an induction ceremony. At a point we were told to wait to be summoned individually. I was so exhausted that I fell asleep. The wait was several minutes. The rest of the Scouts were called to the ceremony. Sometime later, I awoke with no one around and panicked in the dark. Finally, a leader came looking for me and carried me to where everyone was sleeping. The next morning, we had a good breakfast and headed to Franklin. I did not get the Brotherhood or Vigil ranks.

I served only three hours of detention while at BGA. Johnny Wilson and I got to scuffling over a quarter that I had dropped on a classroom floor. Bunny Akin, Mr. B as students called him, gave me three hours, none to Johnny. After class I asked him why I got time and Johnny didn't. He replied, "I need my lab cleaned and you will do a good job." (If you worked off your time you got double credit). Lesson learned. Life is not fair.

Graduation from BGA was a milestone. I was the first of my family to graduate from high school. Next was Vanderbilt!

28

My mother, Susan Lorene Crutcher, holding me in 19 s.

Daddy and Mama Hicks.

I am sitting on the lap of my great grandfather Crafton with my great grandmother Crafton beside him. My mother, Susan Lorene, and my grandmother Mama Hicks are standing.

Mother and I, 1946.

*afternoon visits with my two cousins meant playing on the farm.
That is me in the middle.*

Our Sunday school class, ca. 1950, at Mt. Carmel Cumberland Presbyterian Church. I am standing, third from the right, bottom row.

My grandmother, Mama Hicks, always took me to Main Street to buy my schoolbooks before classes began in Williamson County.

My boyhood dog Tip.

I am sitting beside Mother with my brother Ray and my daddy, Blythe Woodside, at our home.

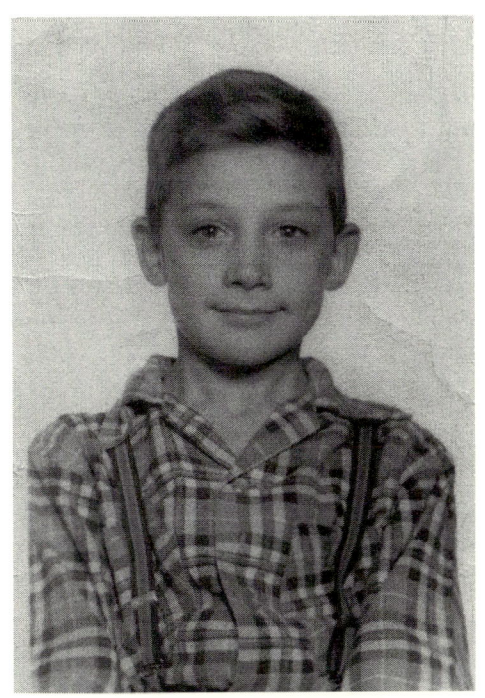

I was a student at Lipscomb Elementary in the early 1950s.

Our family lived on a farm owned by Tom Robinson, near present day Interstate 65 and Highway 96 east (ca. 1957).

Participating in Boy Scout Troop #153 was one of my favorite past times growing up in Williamson County.

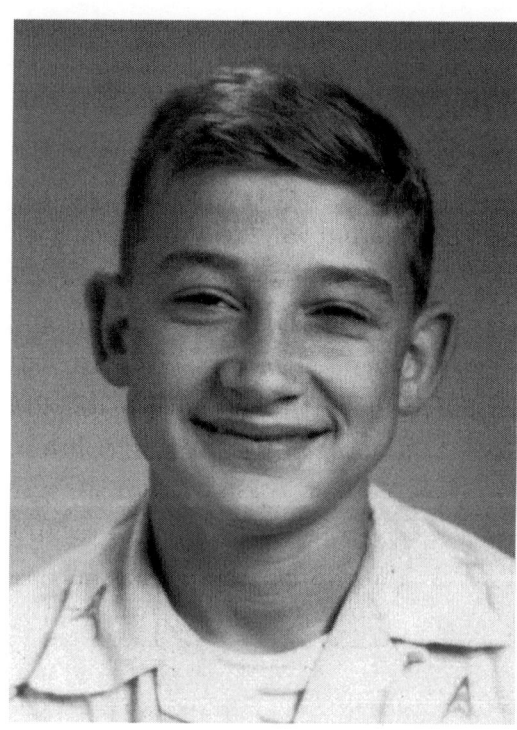

One of my school pictures while attending Franklin Junior High, then located on Canon Street.

Franklin Junior High School, eighth grade class of 1959. I am standing on the second row, third from the left.

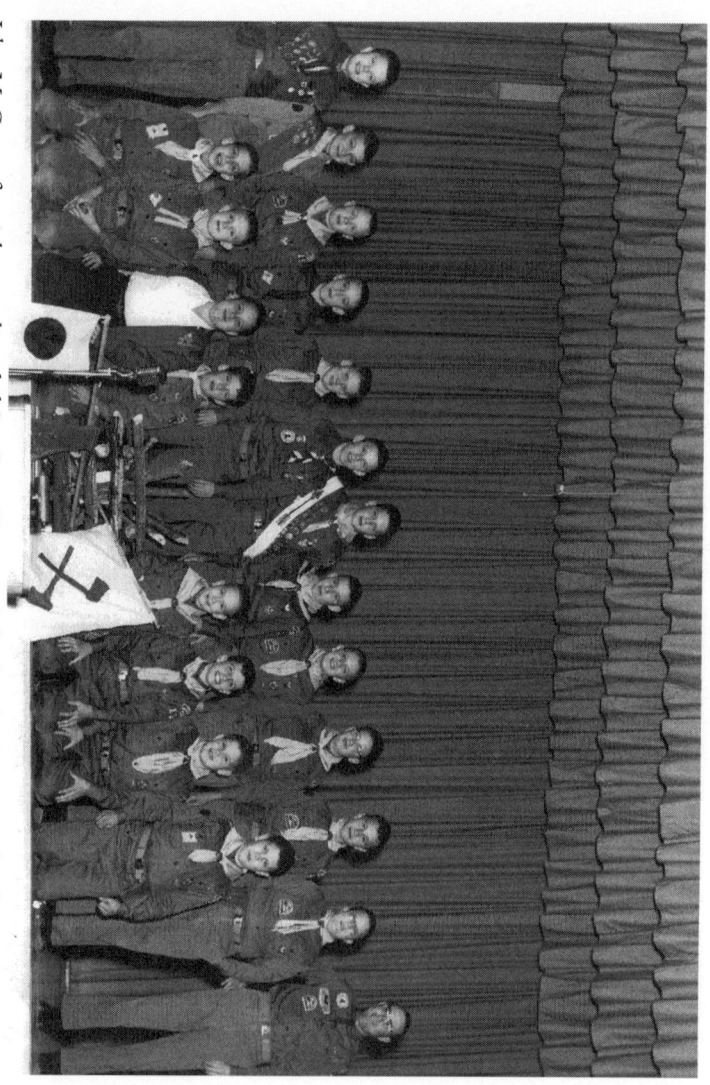

John M. Green, far right, standing, led Boy Scout Troop #153 for decades. I was privileged to be a part of his troop. That's me standing on the back row, second from the left.

Mother was present when I received my Eagle Scout award for Boy Scout Troop #153. The gentleman administering the badge is not identified.

My lifelong friends, John Green, left, and David Moran, right, and I stayed in touch over the years.

The contractor for Interstate 65 took this aerial view about a mile south of State Route 96 east (ca. 1962). The Harpeth River required this bridge. Notice the car in the foreground. It was later demolished.

38

Battle Ground Academy was an important time in my life.
Senior class photo, 1963.

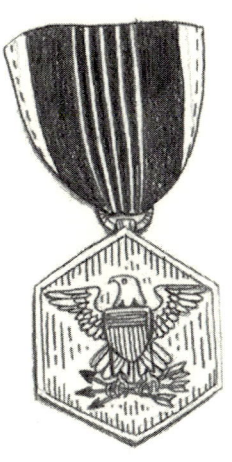

BRIDGING RIVERS

5

TRANSITIONING TO ADULTHOOD

1963 – 1967

THIS PERIOD OF MY LIFE contained my lowest and my highest personal events. The lowest–the death of my mother. The highest– meeting my future wife. More about these later.

I had learned two things in the eighteen years I had spent on the farm: (1) how to raise tobacco, and (2) I needed to do something else for a living. Farming is a good life, but I was not cut out for it. These learnings made me realize that I needed to go to college.

I applied for admission to and scholarships for three colleges– University of Tennessee (UT), Vanderbilt University (VU), and Tennessee Tech. My SAT and ACT scores were good, and I was a National Merit Semifinalist. I felt that I was well prepared for college since I had gone to a great prep school. I was accepted by all three universities.

Two teachers from BGA had taken positions at Vanderbilt:

David Wood, as assistant dean of admissions, and Cannon Mayes, as assistant dean of financial aid. They had firsthand knowledge of my qualifications and potential.

The Tennessee recruiter asked me to meet him at the school's agricultural extension farm in Spring Hill. I had been awarded the University of Tennessee Sears Scholarship. My meeting with the recruiter was very pleasant but brief. We discussed my resumé and the other schools I was considering. He asked about my scholarships; so, I showed him Vanderbilt's offer, which was a large scholarship combined with a small federal no-interest loan from the National Defense Department. After seeing VU's offer, he stated that his job was to recruit for UT, but he had to tell me that I would be crazy if I didn't go to Vanderbilt. After our discussion I chose Vanderbilt.

My first time on the Vanderbilt campus was the Sunday afternoon that Mother and Daddy carried me to my dorm. 'I had been to the Vanderbilt Stadium in 1960 for the Clinic Bowl when BGA won the state championship; but that doesn't count.' We drove there in Daddy's brand new pick-up truck. This was the first new vehicle he had ever owned. Most of my belongings were in the two new Samsonite suitcases that my extended family had given me for graduation. My roommate was my long-time buddy David Moran. I had arrived!

Ten members of my high school class enrolled in Vanderbilt. This was twenty percent of the BGA Class of 1963. Nine of us graduated from Vanderbilt.

The first week at Vandy was spent in freshman orientation. We were required to do some stupid things, like wearing the freshman beanie, and some good things, like socializing with the young women at a freshman football game and at a dance. Just being in class with females was a pleasant experience after four years of an all-boys school. We were tested to see

44

which section of classes we were to be assigned. BGA prepared us well. I was placed in the top English and chemistry classes. This lasted until the semester grades came out, when I was lowered to the regular classes in both English and chemistry.

The first English assignment was to write an essay about an older relative and tell why he/she was picked. I wrote on Uncle Maude, Daddy's uncle on his mother's side of the family, the Wiley's. The next week the teacher started class by saying that he found one essay very interesting for its content and not necessarily its structure. He began reading mine! I had written on the advice Uncle Maude gave me as the two of us chopped tobacco. We took a lot of breaks under the shade trees so I got a lot of advice. I said to myself that I should get an A- or a B+ as a grade. Wrong! I got a C-. It was back to the regular English class in the new semester. I think the teacher was biased against engineering students.

I came to be in the Vanderbilt University School of Engineering due to the advice of Mr. Wood and Mr. Mayes. They told me the school had more money than the School of Arts and Science and the course requirements were the same in both schools for the first two years. I didn't know what I wanted my major to be, but I knew I wanted it to be in science. I enjoyed the engineering curriculum, including the labs. I never considered transferring.

In the sixties, the engineering school had four majors: civil, mechanical, electrical, and chemical. I chose civil because it had a broader scope and had to do with designing buildings and the sites where they sit. My friend David chose chemical engineering; it has to do with things you can't see.

On Friday, November 22, 1963, I had eaten lunch at Rand Hall, the student center, and was headed to an afternoon class. Suddenly, several people started screaming that

45

President Kennedy had been assassinated. Classes were cancelled. I did not show a lot of emotion or remorse. At BGA we were exposed to a conservative viewpoint in governing, which was opposed to that held by the Kennedy family.

The following Sunday afternoon on a bus ride to East Nashville, to visit Mama Hicks, someone announced that the alleged Kennedy assassin, Lee Harvey Oswald, had been shot and killed. This recollection is my first of extreme violence.

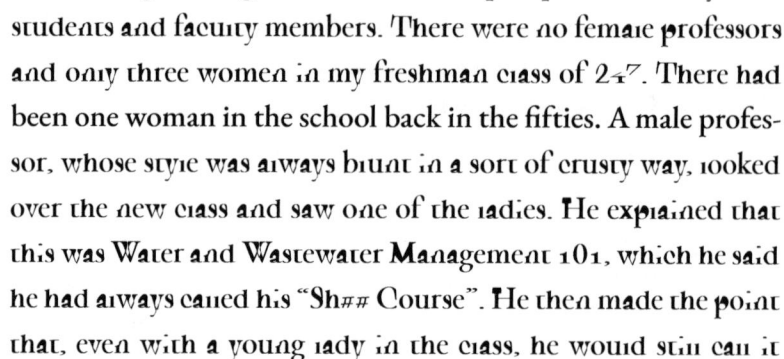

The engineering school was made up of predominately male students and faculty members. There were no female professors and only three women in my freshman class of 247. There had been one woman in the school back in the fifties. A male professor, whose style was always blunt in a sort of crusty way, looked over the new class and saw one of the ladies. He explained that this was Water and Wastewater Management 101, which he said he had always called his "Sh## Course". He then made the point that, even with a young lady in the class, he would still call it his "Sh## Course". Of my three female classmates, only one–Jo Ann Eddy–graduated and became a practicing engineer. She was hit by lightning while inspecting a retaining wall in 2018 and died from her injuries.

I did not join a Greek fraternity. Johnny Green said I couldn't afford one, and, as always, he was right. I did go through rush. I joined an independent fraternity, PSK. In the medieval tradition, the letters represented the Old English words Page, Squire, Knight. The members rented an old house from VU on Pierce Avenue. David and I moved into one of the PSK rooms in our second semester. The rent was cheaper than the dorm rent.

One of our housemates was a large fellow named Dave. He had a bad habit of eating whatever he wanted from the kitchen refrigerator. It didn't matter who the food belonged to. My mother would make me cakes and pies every weekend that I went home to Franklin. I had warned Dave about leaving my food alone but had little success. I did get him to promise not to take it. One Saturday, Mother asked what kind of dessert I wanted to take back to VU. I asked for a chocolate cake with chocolate icing. As soon as I got back to the PSK House, I went to Walgreens and bought a large box of Ex-Lax. Warm milk and half of a box of Ex-Lax makes chocolate icing. Next, I cut a large slice of cake, placed it on a plate, and put it in the refrigerator. I also reminded Dave about his promise not to take my food. An hour later I checked the refrigerator. The cake was gone. I confronted Dave and told him what I had done.

He laughed and said, "You are kidding?" My response was, "It will all come out in the end." The entire house was kept awake that night as Dave got up and headed to the bathroom for yet another trip. We were concerned that he might get dehydrated so we brought him water. The next day he missed his morning classes. After that night, none of my food disappeared from the fridge.

WARNING: DO NOT TRY THIS ON ANYONE! IT IS DANGEROUS FOR THEIR HEALTH AND YOURS IF THEY CATCH YOU.

Academically, my first year was uneventful. I had a near perfect attendance record, turned in my homework on time, and enjoyed most of my classes. Statics and the chemistry labs were my favorites. History of the fine arts was boring. I joined the Army ROTC to avoid taking Phys Ed. The ROTC had an intercollegiate rifle team which I joined. I shot in several matches at VU and earned a varsity letter. I got to take one trip to Ole Miss in Oxford, Mississippi for a match. I still remember how good the catfish was in Bolivar, Tennessee.

My summers were spent measuring tobacco for the United States Department of Agriculture. Farmers were limited to the amount of acreage in which they could grow certain crops. My supervisor was Mary Lois McMinn. I worked from dawn to dusk six days a week. We reporters were paid by the number of farms visited and the acres of crops measured. The primary crop was tobacco, but there was also some wheat, cotton, and corn. I made good money that was put in the bank and used to pay for my VU education. After finishing this job at the end of the summer, I helped harvest tobacco on various farms.

Measuring tobacco was a two-step job. In early summer we reporters would go to the farms and measure how much tobacco had been planted. We weren't supposed to calculate to determine if too much was planted. But the farmers often asked how much they had, and we usually made an estimate. It was the job of Miss McMillan to figure the official acreage and have the farmer notified by mail. If the farmer had an excess, he paid a fee to have the tobacco destroyed. A reporter was then sent to witness the destruction. It was usually several weeks between the measuring and the destruction. Normally, the same reporter that measured was sent to witness.

One farmer assigned to me had a farm near College Grove. My first visit to his tobacco patch was in early June. He asked me if he was within his allotment. I made some quick calculations and said, "Yes." (Shouldn't have done that; I made an error.) On

48

the way out of the tobacco field, I commented on his clean and healthy watermelon patch. "You come back in August when they are ripe, and I will give you all you can eat," was his reply.

The farmer had too much tobacco and paid his fee. I was assigned to witness the destruction. The amount in excess was just slightly above the allotment. When I went back to his farm in late July, I was driving a different car and wearing a different hat. He was cordial but restrained. I told him that we wouldn't have to cut down any good tobacco because he had enough small plants on the edge next to the weeds, as well as a small plot that had drowned out. When we measured those places, there was enough to meet the overage. On the way back to my car, I made a fleeting glance over to the watermelon patch and made no comment, but he did.

"That first boy they sent out wanted some of my watermelons. I told him to come back when they were ripe. He's the one that told me I didn't have too much tobacco. The melons aren't ripe yet, but will be in about three weeks. You come back then. If that first boy comes looking for watermelons, I will run him off with this chopping hoe." I didn't go back, not knowing which reporter he would recognize.

One of the reporters was a high school teacher who measured tobacco in the summer. We were instructed by Mr. Richardson, the field supervisor, to keep a notebook with sketches in it to record our measurements. Well, this teacher did this and kept his notebooks year after year. He got lazy and would ask the farmers if their crop was in the same field as the year before. If the answer was yes, he would not measure and just use the last year's notes.

At least one farmer told the truth, but not the whole truth. The farmer did tell the reporter that it was in the same field, but he did not tell him he planted more rows of tobacco. He had planted one-half acre more tobacco than he was allowed. The state of Tennessee field auditors chose this reporter to audit. They discovered what had happened, made the reporter remeasure all the fields assigned to him for no pay, and then fired him. The rest of the reporters, including me, were required to witness the destruction of the excess tobacco on the farms.

I was assigned the farm with the extra half-acre. I made an appointment with the farmer for early morning. With a lot of trepidation, I pulled up in his yard. He was waiting with his tractor and bush hog. His tobacco field had expanded to the point that he had to cut down the half-acre of tobacco ($1000 worth). He looked at me and said, "Get on." I hopped on the tractor. He did not speak to me again. In my presence, he destroyed the tobacco.

Breathing a sigh of relief, I went to my next stop which was across the road. The men there were cutting tobacco and hanging it in the barn. I asked for the crop owner and was greeted by "Who wants to know?" I identified myself and told them that I had come to destroy excess tobacco. The spokesman for the group then said, "I wondered why he brought his gun today." I must have turned white because the man laughed and said he was only joking.

6

THE BEST AND WORST

1964 – 1967

MY SOPHOMORE YEAR BEGAN with more engineering courses and a job as a student assistant to the drafting professor. The second semester my student job changed to grading papers for Dr. Walter Graham, a math professor. Dr. Graham grew up in College Grove and had graduated from VU. I learned that, as a student, he had traveled by train to Nashville daily to attend classes. We got along well.

Now begins the saga of the best thing that has happened to me. In late November 1964, Mother called me to ask if I had plans on December 23. When I told her I didn't, she explained that Mary Lois McMillan had called and wanted me to take her sister, Joyce, to the Franklin Girls Cotillion Christmas Dance. I reluctantly said yes. Mother worked in the cafeteria at Franklin High School and knew Joyce. A quick call to my brother Ray, also a student at FHS, confirmed that Joyce was okay. Good

51

enough for me!

As it turned out, Joyce's original date had to go to South America to visit a sick grandparent. His misfortune was my godsend. If he had not gotten called away, there would have been a different "Crutcher clan" today. Then again, maybe someone upstairs may have been calling the shots and we would have gotten together anyway.

Wearing my best flannel suit (a hand-me-down) and Vanderbilt striped tie, I picked Joyce up, sight unseen, at the home of her oldest sister Sara. She gave me a white carnation boutonnière. I don't remember if I gave her a corsage. It was love at first sight! The song that was playing when we were dancing and had our first kiss was "Strangers in the Night". Her friends could tell that we were in love!

The next day, I called and asked her out for our New Year's Eve party at the DSK House at Vanderbilt. Her parents said it was okay for her to go; however, they were hesitant since she was a senior in high school going to a campus party with a college sophomore. We dated for the rest of her senior year.

Joyce had planned to attend the University of Tennessee in the fall, but she changed her mind and went to George Peabody College for Teachers which was across the street from Vandy. Could it have been that she wanted to be near to me? I think so. We have continued to be together for fifty-seven years and still counting!

In February of 1966, the low point of my life came. On Saturday, February 12, I came home from Vanderbilt. Ray picked me up from the Franklin Interurban bus stop on the Franklin Square and told me that Mother had been in the hospital since early morning. We drove to the hospital and went straight to her room. She was having extreme pain in her lower abdomen and was heavily sedated. Mother recognized me and squeezed my hand. That was the last time I saw her alive. She had not been seen by a doctor. Her doctor was making an emergency house call out in the county and was communicating with the nurses by phone. My Aunt Robbie and, maybe, Aunt Annie Mae and Mama Hicks were also there in her hospital room along with Daddy and Ray. The nurses were not nice or helpful. Aunt Robbie sent Ray and me home.

Late in the afternoon, we went back to the hospital; still, no doctor. Mother was in a coma from the pain medicine. I went to see Joyce, and she came back to the hospital with me. When we went to Mother's room, we were told that she had died. The McMillans came to pick up Joyce, and we all went home.

The next day, Sunday, was a continuation of the nightmare. Daddy asked me to help him deal with the funeral home and the arrangements. Daddy wanted the service as soon as possible; so, it was planned for the next day, a Monday. We picked out the casket and vault. It was like buying a new car. The man at the funeral home showed us the top of the line then came down to something practical. Daddy selected the pallbearers; we were ready for the visitation and funeral. To this day, I dislike funeral homes.

The funeral was held on Monday in Franklin. Mother was buried in Mt. Carmel Church Cemetery at Duplex near Spring Hill. She was buried next to her sister, Aunt Annie Johnson, who had died in Florida. Many of our friends and neighbors were very supportive and brought food. The best dessert was the German chocolate cake baked by Mrs. Louise Lynch, the first I had ever tasted.

The day after the funeral, Tuesday, Daddy and I handled the business matters at the funeral home. On Wednesday I was back at Vanderbilt to continue my classes. The support of Joyce and her family through all of this was a great comfort to me.

Vandy got to be a good routine—get up, go to classes and labs, eat dinner, study, go to bed. There was one restaurant called The Lazy Susan where my friends and I went once or twice a week. The food was served family-style on a round turntable, hence the name. For a fixed price it was all-you-can-eat. We pigged out! Our housemate Frank was particularly gluttonous. One night he kept requesting food to the point the waitress quit bringing any.

Frank, in his overbearing voice, said to the waitress, "Your advertisement said it was 'all you can eat.'"

She replied, "You have had all you can eat, and I am not bringing anymore."

After Joyce moved to Peabody, the two of us ate at Chambers Steak House across the street from her dorm. Years later Foster and Creighton, my employer, got a job remodeling the Chambers' building and I was the assigned superintendent on that project. The first day of work we found baked potatoes wrapped in foil in a pantry. The building had been vacant at least fifteen years. I started to bring one home to Joyce but thought better of the idea.

Late in the first semester of my senior year, I received a letter from Mr. Mayes, Vanderbilt's dean of financial aid. The letter read, "Congratulations! You have been awarded the National Association of Women in Construction 'NAWIC' scholarship for your final semester." I contacted Mr. Mayes and told him there must be a mistake because I had not applied for the scholarship. He replied that there was no mistake; the women had contacted him seeking the name of a deserving student to award their first ever $500 scholarship. He had given my name. This meant that I didn't have to borrow money to pay for my final semester.

Upon inquiring if there was anything that I needed to do to receive the funding, Mr. Mayes stated, "Nothing. But it would be nice if you attended one of their meetings and expressed

54

appreciation." I contacted the president of the association, Mrs. Anna Bene Freas, and was invited to their April meeting. Since Joyce and I were engaged, Mrs. Freas invited her also. We went to the dinner meeting and met the ladies. I made a short speech. Mrs. Freas, on behalf of NAWIC, gave Joyce a basket of kitchen items. The most prominent utensil was a large rolling pin. Mrs. Freas said that Joyce might need it for baking or to use on me. Joyce still uses that rolling pin when she bakes and, thank goodness, never on me.

Academically, my senior year was uneventful except for one course. I needed an engineering elective for my last semester to fulfill the course credits requirements. My counselor advised taking a public health course. He said the class involved some boring reading and some boring lectures; however, there were only two tests—a mid-term and a final. The professor had been teaching this course for years. He was known for not cutting any student slack over the grades or attendance even if they needed to pass the course to graduate. I went to class and read most of the textbook, but I did not put in a lot of time and effort.

After taking the mid-term, I was shocked to receive an F, the first failing grade I had ever received in my sixteen-year academic career. I knew the challenge I was facing. One test would determine my grade, and I had to score high enough to pull the F to a D, at the very least.

The thoughts of what would happen if I didn't pass kept me awake at night. I would not graduate, could not marry Joyce that summer, and would not be able to go to summer school because I had to go to ROTC camp. I studied, took the final exam, and waited two days for the results. When I checked the posted grades, I found out I had passed with a C! For years I had that classic nightmare—the one where you forget that you have enrolled in a course, which means you don't attend the course.

Life got much better after my brush with a failing grade, but also more hectic. Joyce was finishing her sophomore year at Peabody and preparing to take a year off to earn enough money to finish her degree. She didn't qualify for a National Defense Loan like I had received, because her parents owned a farm. It was March when she and I discussed all of this. We decided to get married. I (we) went to visit Mr. and Mrs. McMinan to ask for permission. There were no objections from her father, at least that he stated; he didn't say a word. Her mother said that she had hoped Joyce would have finished college. I promised her that she would. Joyce did go on to graduate.

I graduated from Vanderbilt on June 4, 1967. Army ROTC Basic Camp was to be between a student's junior and senior year. I had asked that mine be delayed until I graduated so that I could work measuring tobacco. My deferment was approved in 1966; I went to camp in 1967.

I rode with three other students to Fort Bragg, North Carolina. My hair was cut short. But when I walked into my assigned platoon barracks and saw the Master Sergeant who I would be reporting to all summer, I slipped out the door unnoticed and went straight to the PX barber shop. I told the barber to cut my hair shorter. Master Sergeant Harold Jordan had a shaved head and a small moustache. Seeing his slick head is what sent me to the PX. As he explained to the cadets, who he sent to get haircuts, "Hair only belongs on a woman's head."

M.Sgt. Jordan and I got along very well. He discovered three things about me: (1) I was getting a commission at the end of the camp; (2) I was going into the Engineer Corp; and (3) I was engaged to be married in August. He appointed me "barracks' engineer," whose duties involved improving the barracks on Saturday morning while the rest of the platoon was out marching on the parade field. I was popular with my platoon because I got to pick an assistant to help me. One Saturday we installed pull-up bars outside the dining hall. Another Saturday we painted the steps to the second floor of the barracks.

Four cadets were assigned to KP (kitchen patrol). This was a tough duty. It started at 4:00 a.m. and went to 10:00 p.m. You washed large pots and pans, ran the dishwasher, cleaned the dining hall three times, etc. There were more cadets in the platoon than there were camp days, so every cadet did not have to serve on KP duty. Since M.Sgt. Jordan made the assignments, I was shocked one day to see my name on the list for KP. I thought I had done something to tick off M.Sgt. Jordan. As it turned out, the day he assigned me to KP was the day the rest of the platoon went on a night exercise and were out until 2:00 a.m. When I got into the barracks at 10:00 p.m., M.Sgt. Jordan greeted me with, "Come have a beer with me." He didn't go on the exercise either.

One day of training was spent at the 82nd Airborne School. M.Sgt. Jordan was an airborne soldier and wanted all of us to go airborne. I paid attention to the classes and learned that the biggest piece of equipment that could be dropped from a cargo plane was a "small" 3/4-ton dump truck. A road grader had to be dropped in two pieces. The instructors didn't explain how you connected the two pieces if they landed far apart. We finished the day by jumping out of mock-ups of planes that were about fifty feet off the ground.

Back at the barracks, M.Sgt. Jordan asked me, "Crutcher, are you going airborne?"

I answered, "No Sarge, I am going to be an engineer officer, and it appears that the only thing an engineer can safely drop is a D-handle shovel."

Surprisingly, he said, "You're right." End of discussion.

Our class of cadets graduated on Friday morning, August 4, 1967, with pomp and ceremony on the parade field. We senior cadets received our commissions as second lieutenants. There is an Army tradition that the first enlisted man/woman to salute a newly commissioned officer receives a $20 bill from the officer. M.Sgt. Jordan made sure he was close by so he could be the first to salute me. I gladly gave him the twenty dollars. We turned in our gear and headed home. At the graduation ceremony I was awarded one of the Distinguished Military Graduate medals. M.Sgt. Jordan recommended me for my effort.

Three cadets from the ROTC camp joined me on the long trek home to Nashville. We drove through Atlanta without stopping except for gas and a quick meal. I needed to be in Nashville early Saturday morning to get a required blood test for my marriage license. At two in the morning, I checked into a motel room, slept a few hours, and called Joyce at six to come and get me. She came and we went to Marchetti's for breakfast. Joyce was beautiful! She had been sunning for six weeks; the tan was becoming. After breakfast we went to Dr. Ballard's office on Church Street to have my blood drawn.

Joyce had a busy summer. Her brother, Bryant, married Jane Hall in July. She was a bridesmaid in their wedding, so that meant attending bridal showers and teas for Jane, in addition to those held for her. She also took care of planning for our future housing together. She rented a one-bedroom apartment for us on White Bridge Road. Thank goodness it was furnished because we had nothing.

The week before the wedding, I applied for a temporary job with the Tennessee Department of Transportation ("TDOT") as a surveyor's helper. Because I had orders to go on active duty in the Army in November, I could not take a permanent job. My application was reviewed with the decision that I was over-qualified for the job. TDOT did, however, have openings in the training program. I was up front about my future commitment to the Army, making sure to ask if I was obligated to work for

TDOT after I finished my military tour of duty. I was not. The department made me an offer with Tennessee's Traffic Study Division, which I accepted. Fortunately for us, the job was in an office four blocks from where Joyce worked. It started the week after our wedding.

On August 12, 1967, my family and the McMillan family came together at the First Methodist Church on Fifth Avenue in Franklin, Tennessee to witness and celebrate our marriage. Mary Lois, Joyce's sister, hosted the rehearsal dinner the night before at her apartment. My brother Ray was best man. Johnny Green, my former Scoutmaster; Kenneth McMillan, Joyce's brother; and my friends, Ronnie Simmons and Jim Proffitt, were groomsmen. Joyce's sister, Debbie McMillan 'Barrett', served as maid of honor. Mary Lois McMillan, her sister who introduced us, and Janice Hughes 'Swartz', a cousin, were bridesmaids. Melinda McMillan 'George' and Jim Warf, Joyce's niece and nephew, respectively, completed the wedding party. They were our flower girl and ringbearer.

After the reception at the church, we left in my Dad's truck to go to a barn on Mr. Robinson's farm to retrieve our '53 Chevy. When we started to pull out of the barn to head to Nashville, the car would not move. It had been tied to a post with a rope! This slowed our escape a little, but we did get a big laugh out of all of it.

We spent the first night of our marriage at the new Ramada Inn in Nashville. We considered going to Kentucky's Mammoth Cave, but instead decided to stay in Nashville. Joyce was due at work on Tuesday, so we opted for a quiet dinner at Rachel's, which was a very nice restaurant located near President Andrew

Jackson's Hermitage Plantation. An evening movie at the Tennessee Theatre completed our first day of marriage. On Monday we settled into our apartment on White Bridge Road.

Soon after we married, I traded our car in on a newer model, a 1962 Chevrolet Impala. It had an automatic transmission whereas the '53 had a stick shift. This made Joyce happy. Most days we left the car at the apartment and rode the bus downtown. Not only did we save gas expense but also parking fees. We usually carried our lunches but would eat together about once a week at a restaurant close to where we worked. Satsuma and B&W Cafeteria were our favorites. Our anniversary of one month of marriage was celebrated at the Blue Hawaiian Restaurant down the street from the apartment.

As planned, we moved out of our White Bridge Road place in November when I went to Fort Belvoir, Virginia to attend the Engineer Officer Basic Course (EOBC). Joyce moved back home to Franklin and continued working at her job in the actuarial department of Life and Casualty until Christmas. She planned to go to Virginia with me after the Christmas holidays.

At Fort Belvoir I lived in the BOQ (Bachelor Officers' Quarters.) It was tough being separated from Joyce. The highlight of the week was leaving base on a Sunday morning and going to a restaurant in Woodbridge for a western omelette with some of my classmates.

7

LEARNING TO ADAPT IN VIETNAM

1968 – 1969

AFTER NEW YEAR'S 1968, we headed to our one-bedroom apartment in Virginia, which was about ten miles from Fort Belvoir. (I had rented it before I went back to Tennessee.) We left Franklin early in the morning on a warm sunny day and drove late into the night before stopping at a motel in Roanoke, Virginia. When we opened the motel door the next morning, there was a blanket of deep snow with a freezing wind blowing even more. Thankfully, I had a set of tire chains that I put on the car so we could travel in the heavy snow. As we headed to Alexandria, the windshield wipers could hardly keep up. Snow-plows were out in force to keep the highways open. Finally, after twelve long hours, we pulled into the apartment parking lot. We saw none of the Virginia scenery that day.

Joyce was bored staying at the apartment. I took the car to my classes, leaving her stranded every day. To help break the

61

monotony we bought a television. But our boredom was soon interrupted by a classmate and his wife. Like us, they had just reunited following the holiday break. However, unlike me, the classmate had not made permanent living arrangements for himself and his wife. He had planned to freeload on a captain friend stationed at the fort. That didn't work.

One night, unannounced, the couple knocked on our door and asked to spend the night on our couch after a falling out with the captain. We reluctantly told them that they could. The next morning Joyce cooked breakfast while the wife slept. She got up before we went to class wearing a thin, green negligée—no housecoat. Their Northern accent was further aggravating. The wife laid around all day, not offering to make up their bed or straighten the apartment.

When we men returned from class that evening, Joyce pulled me aside. "They have to go," she said. I understood, so I gave my friend twenty-four hours to make other arrangements. There were other apartments available, but he was too tight to pay the rent. They found another couple to take them in.

We became friends with another married couple more like us. They lived in the same apartment complex; so, Joyce and the wife could visit. One pay day, we splurged. The four of us went to a small jazz nightclub in Georgetown for dinner. It was pleasantly relaxing, mainly because the pianist had a subdued style. He played softly, and it was especially easy to enjoy the conversation and company of new friends. We ultimately stayed a couple of hours, talking and listening to great music. It was a memorable night, even to this day. The husband's first assignment was at Fort Knox, Kentucky, as was mine. We stayed friends as long as we were at Fort Knox but lost track of each other afterwards.

While at Fort Belvoir my field jacket was stolen from a classroom coat rack. It was no big deal except for the fact that it had

62

my monthly paycheck in it! I called our banker, Walter Short, at Williamson County Bank in Franklin and told him the problem. He said that the bank could put money in our account and we could make a deposit later. Whoever stole my coat found the check and threw it in a trash can, and it was returned to me. That experience taught me that establishing solid professional contacts, whether in banking or other areas, is the best course. Jumping around from one bank to another does not build the sort of relationship you will most likely need one day. Lesson learned: Establish solid contacts and don't jump around. Walter handled all our banking until he died in the early 1980s. I have been with Williamson County Bank and its successors since 1961.

Our class had one outdoor exercise in February—one day and night on the shores of Chesapeake Bay. The task was to build a platoon barge by connecting heavy, prefabricated pieces on the water. Many of the pieces were so heavy that it took six of us to lift them. The temperature was so cold that a rope thrown in the water would freeze before we could coil it. We slept in two-man pup tents and ate C-rations for our meals. It was miserable. We returned to camp and were allowed to go to our apartments or BOQ's to bathe and thaw our freezing bodies.

Previously, we had listed our preferences for short-term assignments. My choices were Alaska and Vietnam. After the cold night on Chesapeake Bay, I knew I didn't want to go to Alaska; I changed my preference to Vietnam. (Most of us were going to Vietnam anyway.)

My next assignment was Fort Knox, Kentucky, notable for its storage of the nation's gold. My job was with Office of the Post Engineer. Because I had an engineering degree, I was given a GS-9 civilian slot. I did some design work, but I mainly conducted field inspections of road contractor work on base.

The first order of business was to find somewhere to live. Since it was so easy to find a nice apartment at Belvoir, we assumed that housing would not be a problem at Fort Knox. Wrong! Our first stop was Office of Post Housing. There was nothing available, but we were given the name and location of a few rentals nearby. Our brief search turned up few options; in fact, we basically found what could be described as dumps. These housing options were run down, old, and located off base in a scary part of the rural country. We stayed in a motel in Elizabethtown that night and returned to the housing office the next morning. This time we were given directions to a new trailer park, just north of Fort Knox in Vaney Station. The trailer had two bedrooms. It was almost new and was in a nice park with paved concrete roads. I had to drive about twenty miles to work, so Joyce was stuck. We did have our television and she spent a lot of time washing and ironing my uniforms.

After two months of living in Vaney Station, we were able to get housing on post. We were assigned an apartment in a four-unit complex with a nice backyard. I was able to come home for lunch. We ate a lot of hot dogs and smoked pork chops which were purchased at the DX 'Post Exchange'. Our weekly grocery bill was $17.

I enjoyed being at Fort Knox. We were close enough to Middle Tennessee to make a trip home some weekends, if I could get a weekend pass. Too, I learned new skills from contractors, such as dynamiting rock for roadways, forming for concrete placement, and, the most appealing of all, swapping scrap lumber for fresh baked cherry pies from an Army cooking school near our worksite.

There were some interesting things that happened on this tour of duty. One night, when I was on fire marshal duty, I

64

almost wrecked the fire marshal car by driving too fast on the way to a fire! Thankfully, I managed to dodge a serious accident. Also, during this time, Rev. Martin Luther King, Jr., was killed on April 4, 1968. We soldiers were put on alert to be ready to report to Louisville, if necessary, to confront rioters the night after Rev. King's assassination. We were issued rifles, but we did not have to go.

<hr />

As expected, I got my orders for Vietnam in late September of 1968, less than two months after our first anniversary. The orders were for a desk job at the United States Army headquarters in Saigon. This assignment meant I would be in a secure place with good amenities. The Army stored our furniture at the Smyrna Air Force Base back in Tennessee, and I received a 30-day leave before my departure date.

We decided that Joyce would move back in with her parents until January at which time George Peabody College would allow her to stay in the graduate school dormitory so that she could finish her requirements for a teaching degree. Because she was married, she could not stay in undergraduate housing.

After a sad farewell, I left for Vietnam on November 28, 1968. My itinerary took me first to San Francisco where I boarded a bus to Travis Air Base. While checking in for my flight, I met a former classmate, Kovar. He had been at Fort Belvoir when I was there. We had our last stateside meal at Travis' officer's club and got on a civilian charter plane that went back and forth to Vietnam carrying soldiers.

The first stop for refueling was Hilo in Hawaii. We disembarked, and while we waited, the USO (United Services

Organizations) gave us cookies and coffee. The next stop was Guam, where we refueled. We were now ready for takeoff to Vietnam; however, a flight of B-52 bombers carrying heavy payloads was about to leave to strike North Vietnam, which delayed our flight. Kovar and I sat in adjoining seats on our charter plane patiently waiting and exchanging light-hearted conversation.

The plane landed at Tan Son Nhat Airbase about noon. A sergeant looked at my orders and told me to take the Army bus to the Officer's Replacement Center. I told him that the orders said I was assigned to the engineer's headquarters in Saigon. His reply, "Lieutenant, that slot was filled six weeks ago. Go get on the bus." As we left the airbase, we passed the scene of an accident. A young Vietnamese boy had been hit by a U.S. Army truck. He was unconscious or dead and had bled heavily. Welcome to Vietnam! I learned quickly that there are some things that one absolutely cannot control. I spent two or three days at the replacement center, during which time my new pocketknife was stolen from my locker along with some money. (I was definitely learning by experience.)

Our orders arrived. The five of us, all 2nd Lieutenant Engineers, including Kovar, were placed on a C-130 cargo plane with about thirty other troops. We took off not knowing where we were going. We had drawn assignments in different units since orders were assigned alphabetically by last name. I was assigned to a battalion of the 35th Engineer Group. My company was stationed across the bay from Cam Ranh, near a village, Dong Ba Thin.

It was a few days before Christmas when I arrived, and Bob Hope was scheduled to come in the following Sunday to entertain the troops on Cam Ranh. An officer and a few soldiers had to remain in camp while the company went to see Bob Hope. Since I had just come from the States, I volunteered to be that officer who remained behind. The men were impressed by the legendary show.

I was made platoon leader of a construction platoon that was building a bridge on QL-1, the main north-south road in Vietnam. The bridge site was so close to the ocean that our work on the abutments was limited to low tide cycles. About ten Montagnard men were hired to supplement the work of the American soldiers. Montagnards are a native people of the central highlands of South Vietnam. They lived in the hills west of our camp. We would send a truck to their village to transport them to our camp and worksite. These indigenous people had the authentic miniature pigs, which they butchered for food. They would fish in the stream at lunch break for small catch. These fish were dried in the afternoon and taken home for the family dinner.

The bridge was to be a single span with steel beams for substructure. The beams were to rest on concrete abutments. One of my duties was to procure the forming material and beams from the Army warehouse on Cam Ranh. The operations officer and I wanted to use form ties, but the soldier in charge of the warehouse said they had none. I then asked about the steel beams. Again, I got the same answer, "None in stock." I then pointed out that I had passed some on my way to his office. He said I could have them since they weren't in his inventory books; more importantly, I didn't have to fill out a requisition.

I went to the warehouse of the large civilian contractor, BRJ-RMK, that was close by and asked for the form ties. Though they did not have the length I needed, they gave me the same quantity in a longer tie. We sent a low-boy trailer to pick up the steel beams, and had our shop cut and weld the ties. Fortunately, a Fort Belvoir classmate drove by our work site and gave me some new tools to go with our air compressor. One of the tools was a chainsaw, which we later used to cut the heavy timbers for the bridge deck.

When it was time to mix and place the massive amount of concrete needed for the abutments, I had the Montagnard workers charge the mixer by using plywood boxes made to hold an exact amount of cement, gravel, and sand needed for each batch of concrete. Placing started early one morning and continued until the mixer motor quit. By the time it was repaired and restarted, it was dark. The company operations officer wanted us to finish the concrete pour so that there would not be a cold joint in the abutment. We were outside our camp, so we had the Army of Vietnam (ARVN) troops provide security to protect us from the Viet Cong. Meanwhile, a firefight was going on about two miles from the worksite. We could see the rockets and tracer rounds. We kept on working.

During our work that night, one of the enlisted men was injured when a crane bucket fell on him. A medivac helicopter was called, and the soldier was airlifted to the hospital on Cam Ranh. Thankfully, he was not seriously hurt and returned to the site a few days later. That was a long day and night!

The work experiences I had with this company were of great value to my professional career, but there were also plenty of memorable events that granted me some unexpected opportunities. Ever since reading *Robinson Crusoe* as a young boy, I had wanted to climb to the top of a coconut palm to cut a coconut. There were several palm trees in our compound; so, up one I went with a machete. The climb was successful. Peeling the hull from the coconut was difficult, but the reward was well worth it—fresh coconut milk!

Another new experience occurred while riding through the jungle. Among the dense roadside growth, I spied some bananas growing and asked my jeep driver to stop. I pulled three or four off and went back to the jeep. It was not what I expected. I took one bite after peeling it and found the fruit that looked so good from the road had not ripened. It actually tasted like a green persimmon back in Tennessee—another lesson learned.

My jeep driver, Ayers, always had a smile on his face and a bounce in his step. I asked if he was so happy because he was a short timer (one who was getting close to finishing his Vietnam tour). He explained, "No, I have just gotten in-country and have been assigned to the engineers rather than the infantry."

I learned that assigning new in-country infantry soldiers to other Army branches until they were needed for combat was a standard practice. The men were subject to transfer to an infantry unit at any time.

One of my enlisted men, Bell, was notorious for disappearing after lunch break. I would look high and low for him. After a couple of weeks, Ayers confided in me that Bell would hide in an empty wooden shipping box, pull the top over his body, and sleep all afternoon. I started carrying nails and a hammer in the jeep, hoping to start nailing the top shut while he was in it. He probably would have started screaming, but, if not, I would have continued nailing it shut and proceeded to have the box thrown into a truck to be hauled to the dump.

I never did catch Bell. His job had been to drive a two-and-a-half-ton truck. This lasted until he sped through a village and hit a Vietnamese grandfather driving a cart being pulled by a water buffalo. The grandfather and grandson were injured, the cart destroyed, and the buffalo killed. Bell was court-martialed and demoted to private.

Another soldier with a good attitude and constant smile was a bulldozer operator. I asked him the same question I asked Ayers.

"Are you a short timer?"

He told me that he was on his second tour in Vietnam and that he planned to re-enlist for a third. I said, "You must like the Army."

His reply was, "It's better than fifteen years in the Federal Pen."

He went on to explain his situation. In his not to distant past, he had stolen a trailer truck in Atlanta and was headed to New York to hock the rig, having no idea what was in the trailer. The rig broke down just outside of Washington, D.C. When the highway patrol stopped to help him, they discovered he had stolen the truck. The federal judge gave him a choice of a fifteen-year prison sentence or five years in the Army.

After hearing his story, I said, "You don't get fifteen years for stealing a truck."

He responded, "You do if you stole the paper that was used to print the money." The cargo in the trailer was paper stock for the Federal Reserve printing presses.

After our company was deactivated, he volunteered to drive a dozer with a Rome plow for a land clearing company. This was a very dangerous job since they were clearing trees and brush alongside the roads so the Vietcong could not ambush the troops traveling the roads. The Vietcong would attempt to attack the dozer operators with grenades. I have often wondered if he made it through the war in one piece.

The ARVN was the security force that protected us. One night the warrant officer in charge of the motor pool asked if I wanted to go on a night ambush for Viet Cong. I declined. I didn't trust the ARVN troops, and my job was to build bridges. I wanted to go home to Joyce, and, with that in mind, I was not going to take any unnecessary risks.

After the bridge was finished, the men, following tradition, wanted to throw the platoon leader in the river. However, we were so close to the South China Sea that they had to wait for the tide to come in so there would be enough water.

When the company was deactivated all of us were reassigned to units scattered throughout central Vietnam. Our captain wanted me to go with him to a combat engineering company supporting the infantry near the Cambodian border. They were mainly building artillery bases. I didn't tell him no; neither did I tell him I had gone to the 35th Engineer Group's headquarters at Cam Ranh and asked a Belvoir buddy in S-1, personnel, to send me to the best construction battalion on the coast. I got my orders for an engineer battalion at Tuy Hoa, north of Cam Ranh.

My transfer was in February. This was the beginning of the monsoon season. The sun would be shining in the morning, clouds would start coming in around ten, then rain would arrive before three o'clock, and continue until midnight. This made for a lot of wet clothes and damp, moldy barracks. It also created a lot of muddy road work. I was assigned to a company that was upgrading a French-built road so that it could carry the heavier loads.

My platoon had a section of road that had to have more gravel placed on it and better ditches on the sides, as well as a realignment at one point. I got the opportunity to improve my problem-solving skills, although at the time I didn't know that was what I was doing. The ditches had to be built in the swampy land that was lower than the road. We had to remove thick mango bushes and deep roots. The monsoon rains made the ground too soft to support the dozers.

The machine, a Gradall, that could stay on the roadway and clear the ditch was broken. I had heard about other units using Bangalore torpedoes to create ditches. We tried them and they worked. They made a perfect 1-foot-wide, 3-foot-deep ditch. Bangalore torpedoes were intended to be used to blow gaps in

71

enemy barbed wire fences, but we worked with what we had.

When we began the road realignment, part of the job was the removal of a rock bluff, which became a project of its own. We tried to break the rock into small pieces using air-driven chisels. This was too slow; therefore, we drilled holes in the rock and blasted with dynamite. Because I had been fascinated with dynamite since watching the building of Interstate 65 as it came through Mr. Robinson's farm in Tennessee, I took the lead in the rock blasting. One of the enlisted men trained in blasting was utilized to load and shoot the dynamite. Important things I had learned at Fort Belvoir's demolition school were now invaluable:

(1) Double fuse all shots.

(2) Allow a foot of det (detonation) cord per minute of burn.

(3) If the fuse goes out, wait five minutes before going to check it.

(4) The man who lights the fuse is the one who has to go check a burned-out fuse.

I had the trained enlisted man light the fuses. One shot failed to go off. It was an anxious ten minutes as the soldier crawled to the fuse, grabbed it, and threw it away. Several of the other troops and I watched from a safe distance. Later, before I left Tuy Hoa, I had another dynamite experience (more about that later).

While working on the roads, we took some breaks to do things like shooting grenades in the streams to stun the fish, so the local people could go in the water to catch them as they floated to the top. Once, we took target practice with our M-14 rifles (we were some of the few troops that were not issued M-16 rifles) by shooting at abandoned concrete telephone poles. The intent was to make them fall over. We bought warm Cokes from

72

the local kids who had stolen them from the Army supply trucks. Hey, their family had to make a living!

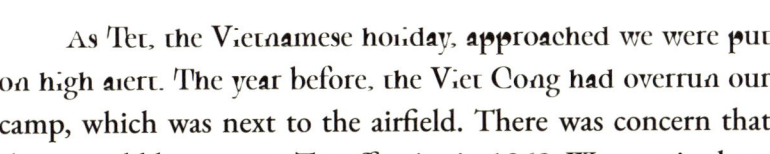

As Tet, the Vietnamese holiday, approached we were put on high alert. The year before, the Viet Cong had overrun our camp, which was next to the airfield. There was concern that there would be a repeat Tet offensive in 1969. We practiced going to the perimeter berm to fight. This took several hours each night. After working all day, this was exhausting. We were glad when Tet ended without an attack and we were taken off alert.

I met an older civilian at the Officers' Club who had a contract to help maintain the battalion asphalt plant. He lived in Vietnam full time and told us he had a Vietnamese wife. He did not disclose where he lived. He did travel around Vietnam to various asphalt plants and was suspected of being a CIA agent. He was low key and likeable.

On Sunday afternoons we could go to the local village. There you could buy souvenirs and fake antiques. I still have a couple. There were also small restaurants. One was Korean that served good food, but it was spicy hot. They had a clear soup and noodle dish, both set me on fire.

One day a soldier was hauling a bulldozer on a low-bed trailer through a village. He had failed to tie the dozer down to the trailer. When he made a sharp turn, the bulldozer fell onto the road. I was assigned to investigate to see if he was negligent and should be disciplined. I determined that he should be court martialed for failing to follow proper procedure, i.e. to tie down equipment. My recommendation was not accepted by the officers above me, and he was only reprimanded.

After three months in Vietnam, I got a notice that my

television, which had been shipped to Saigon, was in Cam Ranh. I caught a military flight to retrieve it. This was during the time of the Tet alert, and a short trip to Cam Rah was a good break. I was on the last flight of the day and had to spend the night there. I got my TV, had a good steak dinner at the Officers' Club, and settled into a peaceful night's sleep in the BOQ (Bachelor Officers' Quarters).

Sometime after midnight I was violently awakened by a large explosion. Outside was dust and the smell of gunpowder. Troops were running around; some were shooting out the security lights. We had been hit by a North Vietnamese long range rocket. It could have been shot from thirty miles away. After drawing a rifle from the armory, I spent the rest of the night in a bunker. The next morning my television and I were on the first plane back to Tuy Hoa.

While at Tuy Hoa, I drew the duty of pay officer. This involved traveling to Dalat to pay the men who had relocated. I had gotten a letter from Joyce saying that Pete Mosely, her sister's bother-in-law and an infantryman in Vietnam, had been injured. He was in the hospital in Nha Trang. I was able to stop in Nha Trang to check on Pete; however, when I got to the hospital, I was told that Pete had been air-evacuated to Yokohama, Japan the day before my arrival. He was the machine-gunner on an armored personnel carrier (APC) when it was hit by a rocket propelled mortar (RPM).

When Pete was injured, he was carried to a medevac helicopter. The copter was then shot from the sky. Pete had head injuries and his left arm severed. He recovered enough in Japan to be sent stateside. After spending a few days at home, he was transferred to the military hospital at Fort Gordon, Georgia. After many operations he was able to return home. Today, Pete lives on the Mosely farm in Noleasville, Tennessee and is very

74

active in his community. Fortunately, I see him at local festivals and family gatherings.

Our battalion was finishing upgrading the road and moving to Dalat in the central highlands of Vietnam in April 1968. There was a large, French-built bridge in the section of the road we had upgraded. Our engineers had determined it was adequate and did not need to be replaced. The Vietcong engineers disagreed. Since we used the bridge during the day and they used it at night, the bridge was blown up one night so that we would have to replace it.

The next morning at daybreak, all resources were used to reconstruct the bridge. This was the only road along the coast. With the bridge out, all traffic was halted, including bicycles, motor scooters, and ox carts. The South Korean troops had been providing crucial security protection throughout the war. I am sure the U.S. Department of Defense had made an agreement for this with the South Korean Government. It allowed their troops to be trained with pay in actual combat in a foreign land. Troops from Australia and Thailand also aided American troops in Vietnam, but my experience was only with the South Koreans.

With security from the South Koreans that morning, our plan was to install large steel culverts, eight feet in diameter. The culverts came in pieces that had to be bolted together. The dozers and the cranes with clamshells cleaned out the riverbed. The culverts were set and shot rock was hauled to backfill them.

But before the roadway was finished, a detachment of South Korean troops tried to go over the culverts in their armored personnel carriers (APC). One of our dozers had to block the APC. The South Korean soldier manning the mounted 50-caliber machine gun turned it toward the dozer operator. In a quick response, the operator raised the dozer's blade as a shield and proceeded toward the APC, forcing the South Koreans to back up to avoid being pushed in the river.

It was something to witness. I am not certain why the APC attempted to infringe on the newly built culverts, but our dozer driver handled the situation. The South Koreans played an important role in our protection, and we were usually glad to have them looking out for us against the Vietcong, mostly because they were mean and vicious. If they captured a Vietcong, they shot him/her, rather than send them to prison. They were rumored to cut off the ears of the Vietcong soldiers they killed for souvenirs. American troops and South Koreans had separate compounds. On one occasion, I swapped my c-rations with a South Korean in exchange for his field rations. The spicy fish in his main course pack tasted a whole lot better than what we had been eating.

The bridge reconstruction was completed, but not without some additional excitement. While we were onsite, my jeep driver got in the water and had a foot-long blood sucking leech attach itself to his leg. We had to stick a burning cigar on the leech to get it to get off the leg. The man was treated at the field hospital after we got back to camp.

While at Tuy Hoa, I was selected for a desk job at 35th Engineer Group headquarters at Cam Ranh. My duties included some design work, checking bills of material for projects, and making field inspections throughout the 35th Group. It was a good assignment; I was happy to get it.

76

I almost got seriously injured, however, the day before I was to report. I was in my BOQ killing time when a radio call came in saying that a helicopter had crashed and the wreckage had to be destroyed. This was to prevent the Vietcong from getting the material and making it into something to hurt our troops. The copter had gone down in a steep ravine; therefore, the wreckage could not be airlifted out. I checked out two cases of dynamite, det cord, fuses, a hammer, and a wrecking bar. It was a short helicopter flight to the wreckage.

The downed pilot was not seriously injured and had been airlifted to the field hospital. The troops already had one case of dynamite. We took all of the dynamite to the wrecked chopper and prepared it for destruction. Helicopters are made of honeycombed aluminum floors and sides. It was easy to punch holes in the floors and walls. These holes were used to hold the sticks of dynamite. Det cord connected the dynamite sticks. The det cord was detonated by fuses set off by fuse cord. The fuse cord burned at a rate of one foot per minute. We placed all the dynamite in the chopper and even on the blades. It was essential that the rotor mechanism be destroyed to avoid it being captured by the North Vietnamese. We put fifteen feet of fuse cord on two separate fuses. This was to give us fifteen minutes to get away. We lit the fuses and ran. We were about one hundred feet from the wreckage when the chopper exploded!

Our best guess was that the fuse cords flipped over one another and short circuited the burn. I dodged one helicopter seat and was deafened by the noise. We went back to the site and could find no metal remains. It was like the helicopter had been vaporized. All the grass and bushes were gone, leaving a bare spot. The outcome of this incident could have been different, and there would have been no Crutcher clan.

The best assignment of my tour in Vietnam was Cam Ranh. I had a single room in the BOQ, the food was good in the mess hall, and the Officers' Club was good. More importantly, I had a meaningful job with qualified enlisted men to perform our duties.

My room was in a one-story building. The floor was concrete. The outside wall was plywood six feet high. Above that there was a wire screen with wooden sun deflectors. These were four feet high. The inside walls were also plywood. Vietnamese mama sans (a nickname service-men gave to older women who worked as domestics) were assigned to clean our quarters, make our beds, and wash and iron our clothes. We paid them cash in local currency.

One day I caught a foot-long iguana and tied one end of a string around his neck and the other end around my bunk leg. These reptiles were plentiful and known to eat mosquitoes. I hoped it would keep my room mosquito-free. One day at lunch I went to the BOQ and was confronted by my mama san and her Vietnamese supervisor who could speak English. It seems my mama san saw the string going under the bed and got curious. It did not take much pulling on the string to get the iguana to come out. The supervisor translated to me that mama san said either the iguana goes or she goes. I chose to have a clean room and to swat mosquitoes.

I ate most of my meals in the dining hall. Officers were charged for their meals; the cost was taken from our monthly paycheck. The food was delicious. The eggs were cooked to order, bread was freshly baked, and the vegetables did not taste like they came from a can. The meat was top quality.

The Officers' Club was outstanding. Food was also served there at night as was all sorts of drinks. There were pool and ping pong tables and a television behind the bar where we watched the Johnny Cash Show. The familiar Nashville sound made me homesick. Every month or so a touring band would come and perform. I remember one Saturday night when a Filipino band performed. They tried to imitate the rock and roll and soul bands we enjoyed back in the States, particularly The Supremes.

Later that night after the show, some of the officers were misbehaving and disrespecting the 35th Group's shield. They were called into the colonel's office the next morning and told that if they misbehaved again, they would be reassigned to a land clearing company, a dangerous position. I was not a part of that group.

One of my assignments was to design an underground command bunker that would stop the largest Vietcong/North Vietnamese rocket. In order to prepare the design, I needed the dead and live loads. The dead loads were those that were permanent, i.e. did not change. The live loads were those that were temporary. The dead load on this structure would be the weight of the concrete roof, plus the sand over it. The live loads would be the furniture and equipment on the concrete floor and walls, as well as the load created by the impact of the rockets or bombs. The load from the furniture and equipment was minuscule and could be ignored. Design data on dead loads, and most live loads, was available in engineering manuals. There was no data on what live load a rocket or bomb hit would create. I used my best judgement and designed an 18-inch-thick-roof. The command center was built according to my design. I have wondered if it was even used.

One of the enlisted men working under me focused solely on ensuring that the requisition for the Bill of Materials (BOM) was accurate. If he questioned the material or quantity for a project, he would bring it to me. The reasons for an inflated request could be (1) they plan to sell the material on the black market; (2) it is replacement material used for another project; or (3) they plan to give it to friendly local Vietnamese to to build houses. If I agreed that the request was inflated, I would request a written explanation from the field officer making the request. Based on the explanation, I either approved, rejected, or modified the requisition.

One of the field inspections was of an Army airfield at Phan Rang about 125 miles south of Cam Ranh. I went with Lt. Soider, a fellow classmate when I was at Fort Belvoir, whose company would be performing the work. We were to determine how many metal panels used to cover the runway needed to be replaced. The trip started as planned. Early in the morning, we drove from Cam Ranh across the bay to the Army airfield. We had booked a one-hour flight to Phan Rang. We flew in an Army Dehavilland Beaver, a single engine fixed-wing airplane that could carry up to six people. We left orders for a return flight in four hours.

We met the officer in charge of the airstrip, inspected the panels that needed to be replaced, and estimated the number of panels required. It was early afternoon when we finished, and we were ready to head back to Cam Ranh. We waited a couple of hours; no plane came to carry us back. At that point, we asked the airstrip commander to radio the Cam Ranh airfield to check on the flight. The dispatcher said there were no orders for a return flight, but he promised to send one as soon as he could.

It was about three hours before we were in the air headed

to the Cam Ranh airstrip. We were flying up the coast at elevation of about 1700 feet and a couple of miles off the coast. As we were passing a large forest used by the North Vietnam troops and Vietcong, the pilot and co-pilot started looking out of the plane and engaged in heavy discussion. Since we were in the back seats, the roar of the engine prevented us from hearing what they were saying. The forest was regularly bombed by the U.S. Air Force, so I speculated that our pilot had been alerted by radio that bombers were coming in to drop their bombs.

Suddenly the plane turned upon its side! It flew that way a short time then settled back into a straight course. Lt. Soider and I had strapped on parachutes before we left Phan Rang; now, we were checking the straps. About the time our hearts returned to a normal beat, the plane rotated 90 degrees in the other direction. Soider was reaching for the door! I shouted to him. "We aren't high enough for the chutes to open!" The plane settled down and we continued on to the airstrip. It was now dark. Our pilots had very little in the way of landing lights.

As soon as we were out of the plane, I questioned the pilot about the flight and asked if I was correct about the bombers. He replied, "No, the co-pilot is new, and I was just teaching him that maneuver."

Most of my inspection trips were by jeep. I carried a M-14 rifle and a short-barreled, government-issued 12-gauge shot gun. It was loaded with #2 buckshot. This weapon was easier to swing from a jeep seat, and the buckshot made a larger close-range shot pattern than a single rifle shot.

A five-day trip to Dalat was probably the best as far as learning about the central highlands of Vietnam. I went by jeep, beginning at Cam Ranh. My jeep driver and I stopped for meals and slept at the various 35th Engineer Group companies that we encountered. After leaving Cam Ranh, we went south on QL-1 to Phan Rang and turned west on Route 27. This road became QL-20 which went to Dalat.

Along the coast Vietnamese farmers were planting rice shoots in the paddies. They were using water buffaloes to pull the wooden plows. Entire families, including mama sans and children, worked planting the rice. Babies and the small children were left on blankets on nearby dikes. Later in the year, when the rice had been harvested, the family would remove the rice grains from the stalks by beating them on the hard ground. The ground had hardened after the monsoon season was over.

Route 27 rose from sea level at Phan Rang to an elevation of 4,934 feet above sea level at Dalat. As retribution after World War II, the Japanese were required to construct a large electric generation plant. The turbines were to be powered by falling water that came down in steel flumes from a lake higher up in the highlands. This was possible because of the elevation change. The power plant was never operational; it appeared to be almost complete. The flumes were in place and electric lines had been run on steel towers away from the plant. The plant was abandoned and anything that was removable had been.

While in Dalat we ate with some other officers at a nice civilian restaurant. The food was excellent: thick steak, some local vegetables, and fresh tomatoes. I didn't ask if the steak was beef or water buffalo.

On a later trip to Dalat I was tasked with evaluating a proposed addition to the airport terminal. I had tea with the airport commander. We discussed the nearby tea plantations which had been owned by French families dating back to the French colonization. He told me the Vietcong had recently overrun one plantation and killed the French owner. I had actually flown there on a military flight, but Air Vietnam, a civilian airline, was also actively using the airport.

Later that spring, I had been given a seven-day R&R (rest and relaxation) for late April. I was to meet Joyce in Hawaii. She was still in class at Peabody but would take a weeklong break from classes. Soon after making our plans, I was asked to swap the date with another lieutenant for a time in June. His wife was pregnant and couldn't travel after May. I made the swap because Joyce would have finished her semester classes by June. The Army handled everything, including flights for Joyce from Nashville to Honolulu and accommodations for us at the Royal Hawaiian Hotel. I flew on a chartered flight from Cam Ranh to Hawaii. The plane was full of other married soldiers going to meet their wives. Needless to say, it was a happy group of men. My flight arrived several hours before Joyce's. I checked into the hotel and went back to Fort Derussy, the welcome center near the hotel, to wait for my bride. We both were exhausted from traveling, particularly Joyce.

The next morning after a good night's sleep we were awakened by a loud "boom, boom, boom!" I jumped out of bed and was trying to get under it before I recognized where we were and that the noise was not from incoming artillery rounds. The noise was coming from pile drivers next door where a new hotel was being built.

Now we were ready to enjoy the sites of Honolulu. Our first interest was exploring our hotel, popularly known as The Pink Palace of the Pacific, or The Royal Hawaiian. It was named for the pink stucco on the façade and its unusual architecture.

Though it was built in 1927, it had been well maintained. The property included a handsome private beach; only the white sand separated it from the majestic blue ocean. We ate several meals, including breakfast, on the outside patio where temperatures were kept comfortable by a cool ocean breeze.

We spent a lot of time at the beach. I tried to surf without much success. But going out beyond the surf in guided war canoes was fun. The Royal Hawaiian had a world-renown luau on the beach. A whole pig was roasted, then served to the guests, making for a memorable meal. One night we attended the Don Ho show at an outdoor amphitheater. After a delicious buffet dinner, we enjoyed the entertainment and the traditional food of the Island. Most of our week together was spent walking through the downtown areas and just enjoying being with each other.

At the end of the R&R, the other soldiers and I went to the Honolulu airport to see that our wives' departure went well. The door on their plane was being shut when a disturbance in the plane occurred. A drunk man had locked himself in the bathroom, and the airline attendant could not get him to come out. Mechanics had to come in to remove the door. Police swarmed the plane. Shortly thereafter, he was escorted to jail. The plane departed for California after the door was reinstalled. It had been delayed two hours.

We watched all of this from the observation deck. Seeing our wives leave for several more months of separation had already made us despondent; this added to the agony. We were a plane full of unhappy troops when we left for Vietnam later that night.

8

DOWN TO BUSINESS

1969

I PULLED OFFICER-OF-THE-DAY duty twice while at 35th Engineer Group headquarters. This required the officer to man the radio transmissions with the field units and awaken the higher-ranking officers if an extremely critical incident occurred, such as a unit being overrun by the Vietcong or NVA 'North Vietnam Army'. This never happened while I was at the Group headquarters, but a more frequent occurrence was the sad duty of receiving radio reports of soldiers being killed by enemy fire. That information was forwarded to the United States Military Assistance Command Vietnam 'MACV' in Saigon. From there it was radioed stateside so an Army officer could go personally to notify the soldier's family. It was crucial that the family receive the news this way. I had one such report to come to headquarters while I was on duty.

One benefit of this duty assignment was the opportunity to

place telephone calls to our family back home thanks to the amateur ham radio operators. These volunteers would patch calls around the world. It took a lot of time, but it was rewarding. I got to talk with Joyce once. I was able to reach her at 2:00 a.m. Vietnam time, which was 1:00 the previous day in Franklin.

Military communications have changed. Thirty years after my days in Vietnam, soldiers in Iraq and Afghanistan could use their cell phones to call their families and send pictures and videos. War is still hell! I am thankful that eighteen-year-olds are not being drafted. Another way we passed the time there was to copy reel to reel music tapes. Many of us bought great tape decks at the PX. Two decks would be connected, and we would copy for hours. The music was nice to hear back in our BOQs.

Once, I pulled the duty to work with several MP troops to clear a Vietnamese fishing village of Army troops. The village was on Cam Ranh and was separated by rows of concertina 'barbwire'. No troops were allowed in the village, but that restriction didn't stop the men from cutting gaps in the wire and visiting the Vietnamese. Some of the troops had relationships with the mama sans that worked on Cam Ranh. This led to the birth of Vietnamese-Americans that were shunned and often sent to orphanages. The MPs did this every night, but with a different duty officer. No one was ever arrested. The MPs always made enough noise on purpose so the men could flee through the concertina.

The currency of Vietnam was and still is the dong. In 1969, the exchange rate was 0.0849 dong per dollar; it took twelve dongs to buy one dollar. US dollars could not be used except on the military bases; however, a black market existed where

Vietnamese and Americans would trade dollars for dongs. This was a large and lucrative business throughout the country because one dollar could buy 200 dongs. In order to stop this black market, the Vietnamese periodically exchanged the old dongs for new. The old dongs had no value except to be used for new dongs at the official exchange rate. The upcoming exchanges were known only by the officials; however, the black-market operators knew several days in advance. The trading of old dongs for US dollars prior to the exchange was hectic.

While in Vietnam, I had one work-related injury. Several of us shared a large office space filled with desks and drafting tables. At the end of the room were three or four banks of flat cabinets used to store large sets of plans. Each cabinet was ten drawers high. One day I was walking across the floor, looking down, and reading a letter. My next memory was lying on the concrete floor and seeing an open file drawer. Someone had left a drawer open, which was a safety violation. As I remember, men were standing over me, checking for injuries. After waiting a few minutes to let my head clear, I was able to stand. I was bleeding from the arch of my nose, exactly the height of the opened file drawer. I was carried to the field hospital for examination and treatment. I had no head injuries, only a cut nose. A stitch or two and a bandage took care of the nose. One of the enlisted men in my unit suggested I apply for a Purple Heart, a medal for being wounded in war. He was being facetious.

One memorable trip was to a base outside of Saigon. One of the 35th units needed a soil testing kit and a surplus one was located at this base. I flew in a single prop plane called a Bird Dog, an apt description since the pilot was the only other person aboard. On the return flight the pilot asked if I liked country music. Hearing that I did, he started twisting the radio dials and, in a few minutes, we were listening to the Grand Ole Opry

Live from Nashville!

Two majors from the Pentagon were sent to Vietnam to re-cruit junior officers to re-up (reenlist) for another tour of duty. My commanding officer, a major, said to me, "You need to go meet with them." I informed him that it would be a waste of time since my mind was made up to leave the Army when my commitment was completed. But he pressed me, saying, "These men were sent from Washington, D.C. just to talk to some young officers. They need to do some interviews. It won't hurt you to go."

Immediately, upon entering the interview room, I recog-nized one of the majors from Fort Belvoir. He was from Co-lumbia, Tennessee, which is twenty-six miles south of Franklin. Each time we met we talked about Franklin and Columbia. He either had a good memory or had been doing his homework. "Lieutenant how are things in Franklin?" were his first words.

I answered, "You will have to tell me, sir. It's been eight months since I've been there."

After a good laugh, we got down to business. They wanted to know what I liked about the Army. I told them that I liked the systems and procedures and the building materials that were available.

One of them asked, "What don't you like?"

My answer was brief. "Spending twelve months in Vietnam, eighteen months stateside, and then another twelve in Viet-nam."

The next round of questions got more to the point. They asked what it would take to get me to reenlist. My answer was, "Promise me I won't be sent back to Vietnam." They told me they could do that. "Now throw in Cambodia, Laos and Thai-land," I replied.

Their answer was clear, "We can't do that."

"Then I am going back to Franklin, Major. Please look me up the next time you come through, and we will have a cup of coffee." After a salute, I walked out the door. We all had smiles on our faces.

I had another offer to reenlist that I actually considered. The Chief Warrant Officer for the Post Engineer of Cam Ranh contacted me directly and asked me to meet with him at his office. I agreed and he sent a jeep for me. The Post Engineer was Colonel Goff, who had been my commander at Fort Knox. He had been reassigned to the same position at Cam Ranh and had brought along the Warrant Officer 4th Class as his assistant.

The Colonel (he may have been promoted to brigadier general) could not meet with me because he was on leave in the States. He had left instructions for his warrant officer to contact me and make an offer. Colonel Goff wanted me to extend my enlistment and remain in Vietnam as one of his senior officers. I would be promoted to Captain immediately as well as given a two-month leave to spend with Joyce. I told the Warrant Officer I would consider it and promised to give him an answer in two days.

The offer was enticing. If I wanted to make the Army a career this was an excellent opportunity. Working under Colonel Goff would advance my career if I did a good job, which I planned to do. After all, Colonel Goff had awarded me my first Army Distinguished Service Medal for my work at Fort Knox. I was not opposed to a career in the Army.

The downside of extending was that Joyce and I would be separated for another long period of time. I didn't know her thoughts on the extension or the possibility of us having an Army career. I could have requested the Warrant Officer to set up a telephone call with her so we could discuss it; I also could have attempted to exchange letters with Joyce about the opportunity.

After twenty-four hours of reflection, I told the Warrant Officer that I did not want to extend. I didn't bother Joyce.

Knowing I was leaving the Army, I got down to the business of looking for a job. I wrote to Mrs. Freas, who was with the National Association of Women in Construction in Nashville, and asked if her husband's construction company had any open positions. In her return letter, she told me that they were retiring and closing the company. She went on to say, however, that one of the NAWIC members, Virginia Frazer, worked for a large construction company in Nashville—Foster and Creighton Company. She told me she believed they might be hiring. Mrs. Frazer set up an interview for the first week of December, 1969.

My military tour was up at the end of November. My replacement arrived a few days early. I briefed him on the job and formally turned everything over to him. I was allowed to take my discharge orders to the replacement center at the airport. If there were empty seats on a flight back to the States, they would be filled with soldiers waiting to go home. This happened often. I was booked on a flight leaving later in the day, but I was bumped by someone with an earlier departure date. I checked into the dormitory to wait for my flight, still hoping for an earlier one. I departed two days later.

Lieutenant Kovar arrived for his flight to the United States. This was not a surprise to me since we had flown to Vietnam on the same plane one year earlier. I hadn't had any communication with him since the C-130 scattered us throughout the country to our respective assignments. Contrary to the talkative Kovar I knew the year before, he was now quiet and withdrawn.

We were booked on the same flight leaving the next afternoon. This gave us plenty of time to talk about our year. In answering my questions Kovar said that he had been assigned as the leader of a mine clearing platoon. Things were going okay until one day his unit was clearing a road when the NVA ambushed them. Kovar called in the Air Force to drop napalm on the enemy. Somehow a mistake was made; the napalm hit Kovar's troops. There was loss of life and serious injuries. The mine clearing platoon was rescued by another platoon.

Kovar was relieved of his command and reassigned to a desk job. This explained his reluctance to talk. We were together until we separated in Seattle. I often wonder what happened to Kovar.

I boarded a chartered Flying Tiger DC8 Stretch jet at seven o'clock in the morning Vietnam time. This was Saturday, November 27. We stopped for refueling in Japan and the Aleutian Islands. Our plane landed at McCord Airbase outside Tacoma, Washington at 10:00 a.m. (PT), Saturday, November 27. We had been in the air twenty hours. Thanks to the international dateline, we arrived just five hours after we left!

The discharge center at nearby Fort Lewis was the most efficient operation that I had encountered in the Army. In less than two hours I had been paid, discharged, and given travel vouchers to Nashville. There was one dispute over my pay that was quickly resolved. The Army pay clerk wanted to deduct the monthly allotment that had been going to Joyce. I had stopped it, as instructed, the month before and showed the clerk the paperwork.

She said, "There must be a mistake. I don't have the paperwork you are showing me. You will get a check for it when the mistake is caught."

"No, you pay me now," I replied. "If I get a double payment the Army will get their money back. But I have no way to get

91

what I have coming." She agreed and cut me a check.

I took the Army shuttle to the Seattle airport and had time for a good steak dinner before boarding American Airlines for Nashville via Midway in Chicago. I was getting very nervous as we made ever tightening spirals in the darkness and fog around the city. I had been flying twenty-six out of the last thirty-two hours. We changed planes and headed to Nashville.

I didn't know what to expect at the Nashville Airport at six in the morning on a Sunday. I had called Joyce from Seattle to give her my arrival time. There were no hippies protesting the war, no family welcoming party, only Joyce, but she was who I wanted to see!

We stopped in Franklin to see the house that Joyce had rented for us. Back home, I got out of my Army uniform for the last time. Mrs. McMillan had her usual Sunday dinner cooked when we arrived at Joyce's parents' house. After a year away from home-cooking, her meal was delicious.

I was a civilian again!

My first date with Joyce McMillan,
1964. I escorted her to the Franklin
Girls Cotillion Christmas dance.

Vanderbilt University, 1967.

We married at First Methodist Church Franklin, August 12, 1967. Joyce's
parents Elizabeth and Ellis McMillan, left, and Mama Hicks, standing beside
me, and my dad, Blythe Woodside, celebrated the occasion with us.

94

*Joyce and I attending the Vanderbilt ROTC
Military Ball, 196?, held at the
National Guard Armory.*

*I served with the
?th Engineer Group of the
U.S. army in Vietnam.*

*Our work on the bridge was never
without challenges, but the project was
completed to specifications.*

The South Korean army provided support to our American troops during the war.
(Courtesy of TSLA/Christopher D. Ammons Collection)

The South Korean army, through their armored "Tiger" tank division,
worked closely with American troops in Vietnam.
(Courtesy TSLA/Christopher D. Ammons Collection)

Reviewing construction plans with one of my colleagues from the 35th Engineer Group in Vietnam. I am on the right.

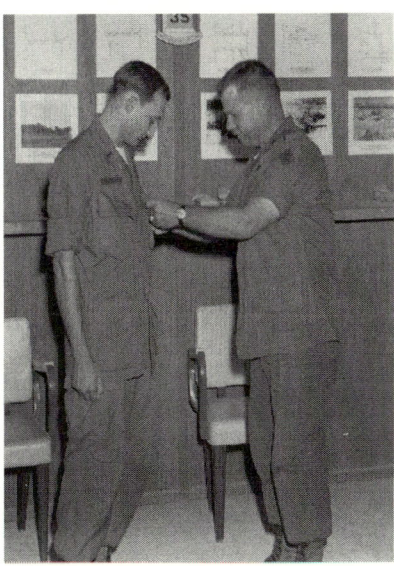

I received my third army Commendation Medal while in Vietnam before returning to the States.

SP4 John P. Vanderhoef, of Portage Wisconsin, sketched this scene of the typical engineering work my 34th Group would have been engaged in during the war. His illustration was featured in the commemorative book I received in 1968 called Engineer Troops Vietnam.

When servicemen completed their duty, they gathered for their return to the States at these headquarters in Cam Ranh Bay.
(Courtesy of TSP4 Christopher D. Ammons Collection)

KICKING SAND

9

REAL LIFE

1970s

THE HOUSE INTO WHICH we were moving was located on Meadowlawn Drive in Franklin. Joyce's sister, Carolyn, loaned us some furniture and dishes until the Army delivered our things that were in storage. Joyce was finishing her last semester at Peabody and getting ready to start her student teaching at West Meade Elementary School in Nashville in January. I was unemployed and continued my job search. Christmas of 1969 was very different, more joyful than the previous year. We visited family, exchanged presents, and felt thankful that we were all together. The two of us celebrated New Year's Eve alone and were ready to go to work and school in the new year.

In early December, I went to a company interview that Mrs. Frazer had arranged for me at Foster and Creighton. While I waited for a decision from that interview, I met with the Tennessee Department of Transportation, where I had worked before reporting to the Army and the U.S. Army Corp of Engineers. Both interviews resulted in job offers; however, the opportunity with Foster and Creighton was the most appealing. I accepted and began my employment at the Nashville firm in mid-December.

Neither Joyce nor I were members of a church although we had both been raised in church. My family attended the Cumberland Presbyterian church. Joyce's family was Methodist. We "church shopped" as soon as we were settled in our house on Meadowlawn Drive. I had attended the Franklin Cumberland Presbyterian Church on West Main Street. Its membership was older, and we were looking for a congregation with younger people our age. We planned to visit the First Presbyterian Church and the Franklin United Methodist Church. We went to the Presbyterian service first. We were welcomed and made to feel at home.

We never made it to the Methodist service. A few Sundays after our first visit we joined Franklin's First Presbyterian. That Sunday we were invited by the Boyce family for Sunday lunch. We went and instantly became friends, a friendship that lasted until their deaths in 2019. Sara, the older Boyce daughter, is presently in Presbyterian Women with Joyce. The First Presbyterian Church has been and still is a major part of our lives.

The man who interviewed me for my position at Foster and Creighton, Roy Slaymaker, became my boss. He was the executive vice president in charge of the building division. Foster and Creighton Company was founded in 1885 and remained in business until 1984. When I began my career there in 1969, it had three divisions: building, paving (concrete), and bridge. The building division had two branch offices, one in Nashville and the other in Lexington, Kentucky. The paving division was

104

completing jobs in Alabama and Nashville when I was hired, however it ceased operations at the completion of those projects. The bridge division had two branch offices–Charleston, West Virginia and Little Rock, Arkansas.

Nashville was an AFL-CIO Union town in 1969. Foster and Creighton, like other commercial contractors, had agreements with the unions. My early work at Foster and Creighton was as an entry-level estimator. I commuted from Franklin to Nashville daily to the company's building at 633 Thompson Lane. The company's building division occupied one wing, where eight men were responsible for the projects. Our team shared the secretary pool of three, all women, with the rest of the company.

Smoking was allowed, but thanks be to God, I never developed the habit. (Tobacco, however, did furnish much of my education funds.) We each had our separate offices, so the smoke was not a bother.

All our work was obtained by what is referred to in the industry as "hard bid." Contractors would determine the cost of a proposed building by estimating the required quantities of materials and labor needed to erect the building. A total bid number was reached after both the overhead costs and the fee (profit) were added.

The contractors seeking the work would submit their bids to the project's owner or architect at an advertised time and place. The contractor with the lowest bid would be awarded the contract. The disappointment of being the second bidder lasted only a few days. The disappointment of turning in a low bid that was too cheap lasted the length of the job.

We worked as a team to bid a job. A senior estimator was in charge of the team. He reviewed the plans and specifications to prepare an estimate breakdown that could consist of more than fifty categories. Each category had numerous items. We had electric calculators but no computers. Each entry had to be checked mathematically. We estimators would be assigned certain categories to determine the amount of material needed. Various tools were used from simply counting items on the plans to using a planimeter to measure areas of earthwork and paving. Pencil sharpeners and electric erasers were essential.

The cost to prepare a large bid would be in the thousands of dollars. It could take two or three weeks, involving three or four estimators. Travel expenses would be an additional bidding cost if the job was bid in another city. Each bid cost someone; there are no "free" bids!

Bid trips to Lexington involved a lot of hard work, loss of sleep, and good food. All bidding was done by the Nashville office even though there was a fully staffed branch office in Lexington. The team preparing the bid would leave Nashville in the morning the day before the bid. We would have a suite of rooms in the Phoenix Hotel and eat great meals at a nearby restaurant. The phone company would install extra phones. These were the days before mobile phones were even imagined. One room was used to meet with subcontractors and material suppliers. Simultaneously, in another room where the extra phones were installed, we communicated with subs and suppliers of materials to get the most and best bids for subs and material. Bid trips meant long days without much rest.

After some hectic moments the bid was finalized. Someone from Foster and Creighton would be at a telephone where the bids were received. This person would fill out the bid form with our information, turn it in, and wait for the bid opening. He would call us back at the hotel with the results. Normally the bids were opened at 2:00 p.m. "EST". By the time we got the station wagons loaded ('SUV's were not on the market'), it was late afternoon. There was little conversation on the drive back to Nashville because most of our team slept. We did, however, stop for dinner before arriving in Nashville at a late hour, even with the time change from EST to CST.

Roy Slaymaker, executive vice president of Foster and Creighton, was the head of the building division. Joe Barnes, Chuck Hutsen, and Warren Lamb were senior estimators. The estimators in 1970 were Bill Bowker, Tad Gardner, Al Turner and me. Roy, and all the senior estimators, gave me OJT ('on-the-job training'). The Foster and Creighton estimating system was highly respected in the industry. Their estimating forms are still used by many construction companies today.

There was a lot of camaraderie among all the employees in the company, not just those of the building division. There was a designated room where we could go for a coffee break at nine in the morning or to eat lunch if you packed one. There was a Shoney's Big Boy restaurant in the next block where several of us would sometimes go for lunch.

The younger estimators would kid or play tricks on Warren Lamb, the oldest estimator. Warren had hearing aids powered by a lavalier that hung around his neck. One day just before coffee break, one of the other young estimators ('not me') concocted a scheme where we would go on break and mouth our words to each other without any sound. As we did this, Warren began to beat on his lavalier, even adjusting the sound control to its highest level. At that point, we began speaking loudly. Warren grabbed his ears and quickly turned down the volume.

Another stunt gave Warren the last laugh. He drove a 1960 Ford Falcon that burned a lot of oil. The car was a light blue color, so we kidded Warren that his Ford must have originally been white but had been turned blue by the oil smoke. One Monday,

Tad and Bill attached a smoke bomb to the car just before quitting time. As usual, when 4:30 p.m. came, Warren rushed to his car. Most of the office staff was watching from the windows. When the car started, smoke billowed from underneath it and Warren came rolling out! He got down on the pavement and inspected the front, back, driver's side, and passenger's side of the vehicle. The observers in the office were beside themselves with laughter.

Coffee break the next day was well attended. Someone asked Warren if he was having car trouble. He cut to the chase and said, "No Bowker and Gardner were playing a prank. I know it was them because neither had enough sense to hook up the bomb by themselves and Crutcher was not here yesterday."

Warren was a good sport, and over the years we became friends. He invited me to view his elaborate home workshop. He had top-quality wood working tools that he had used to build a wood-slatted rowboat and numerous pieces of furniture. He had started a corner cupboard and sold it to me unfinished. I finished it, and it sits in our kitchen today.

We young estimators learned our value to the company. One of my contemporaries had conflicts with the head of the secretary pool, Mrs. Peggy Nelson. He constantly complained to her that his letters were not getting typed as quickly as he wanted. She talked with Roy Slaymaker about his complaints. This resulted in the young man being called into Roy's office. The meeting was short and one-sided.

Roy said to him, "You aren't getting along with Peggy and that has to stop. Peggy's worth to Foster and Creighton is more than yours. I can replace you easier than I can Peggy. If I have to choose between the two of you, you will lose. Now go fix the problem."

The young estimator replied, "Yes sir." The problem was overcome.

I had been bothered by a pain in the right side of my back since 1969. At first it was after drinking beer. By 1970, drinking iced tea would also cause the same pain. In 1971, I went to a urologist and was found to have a partially blocked bile duct emptying the right kidney. This was a birth defect that had caused the kidney to deteriorate to the point it was only functioning at a level of five percent. It needed to be removed before it became infected.

The surgery was major. My right side was cut from my backbone to my navel. The doctor said I would have a lot of pain but would be released from the hospital in a week. That first day of recovery was so painful that I took all of the pain killers allowed. I said to myself that there was no way I could leave the hospital in a week. Two of my fellow estimators came to visit me and reported back to the Foster and Creighton office that I looked terrible. They even questioned whether I would recover. Believe it or not, one week later I left Baptist Hospital.

10

CAVES, DIAMONDS AND PIGEONS
1970s

WHEN I WAS HIRED BY Foster and Creighton, I told Roy Slaymaker I preferred to work in the field. My experiences at Fort Knox, as well as my bridge and road building in Vietnam made me realize that I preferred to be in the middle of something happening, not just pushing a pencil (keyboard keys came later). When the company was selected to build The First American Center in Nashville my opportunity came. I was assigned field engineer for the project.

The First American Center was to be a 28-floor office building in the heart of downtown Nashville. It was planned for the corner of Union and Fourth Avenue, just across from the Metropolitan Courthouse. First American Bank would occupy the first five floors and the remaining twenty-three would be leased as offices. There were two underground levels designed for parking. The existing bank occupied one corner of the site and was

111

to remain until the new bank was opened.

My duties as field engineer were to establish and maintain control lines and elevation benchmarks, check the elevation of the completed excavation, set the elevation of the steel column base plates, and check the steel columns for plumbness.

The project was already underway when I came on board. The buildings occupying the site, other than the bank, had been demolished. Oman Construction Company, the excavation subcontractor, had removed the limestone rock to footing level.

Barge, Waggoner, Sumner, and Cannon, a surveying firm, had established the building control and grid lines and project benchmark. I assumed my duties at this point in the process. I was also responsible for checking and cataloguing new architectural drawings; checking and transmitting to the architect for approval any shop drawings of the subcontractors; and preparing orders for changes in the scope of work. I was responsible for filling out Daily, Weekly, and CPM (Critical Path Method) schedule reports. My top priority was to do whatever Paul Krambeck, the project manager, asked me to perform at a moment's notice.

Foster and Creighton had built a two-story, 2,000-square-foot job site office in the parking lot across Third Avenue from the work site. This was in lieu of using four or five construction trailers. The lower floor was used by the foremen, as well as to store tools and materials. The upper floor contained offices for Paul Krambeck, George Spence, the general superintendent, and Edna Newton, the office manager and payroll clerk, as well as my office. The upstairs offices were divided by walls with doors. There was a narrow porch on the south side which overlooked the construction site.

Working under George Spence were two carpenter foremen, Phillip Burns and Sandy Douglas. Bobbie Hooten was the labor

112

foreman. Depending on the activities taking place, there would be between sixty-five and ninety workmen on site. Two-thirds of those would be on Foster and Creighton's payroll; the remaining third worked for the subcontractors. For a period of time we had two of the early female union laborers working on site. They were truly "Women in Construction"!

Everyone working under George Spence was very helpful to a "green" field engineer. They taught me practical ways to do my job. These were things that were not covered at Vanderbilt's School of Engineering. For example, I learned how to check a dumpy level to see if it was calibrated and how to scribe the centerlines of steel column base plates with a hacksaw. My office duties, along with my field duties, kept me busy from 7:00 a.m. to 4:30 p.m. It was not unusual to put in some hours after 4:30. I enjoyed the work and was never bored or had to look for something to occupy my time.

Compiling the Daily Report, Weekly Report, and CPM Report took top priority. They were carried by Tony, our company courier. Tony made a daily mail run to the main office on Thompson Lane. In addition to my reports, he carried the payroll forms prepared by Edna Newton. It was a union work rule that the foremen had to give out the payroll checks to the workers at quitting time on Friday. If checks were late, the workers were paid overtime to sit and wait.

My reports were used by the main office staff to gauge the progress of the project and assess whether it was within budget. The Daily told how many men worked the previous day and what they accomplished, including the amount of concrete placed. Concrete is placed, not poured. If it is poured, it has too much water in the mix and will not have the strength required by the specifications. The progress of the subcontractors was also included. If a worker was injured, the incident was reported in The Dairy. The Weekly gave the square footage of formwork erected and the tons of stone spread for the sub-base prior to the placement of the concrete slabs-on-grade 'sog'.

The CPM gave the percentage of the activities of the schedule. Foster and Creighton had its own CPM program that they had hired a firm to develop. Roy Slaymaker used this report to create the schedule for the First American project. As soon as my report arrived at the main office, Roy would record the percentages on the schedule. If the project was behind in critical activities, he would meet with Paul to see what needed to be done to get back on schedule. We had top-of-the-line Motorola mobile radios for the entire field crew. The project manager, general superintendent, field engineer and all the foremen had these radios. Edna, the office manager, also had one that she used to dispatch messages throughout the site.

While I was on this project, Joyce was pregnant with our first child. She had a troubled pregnancy with three false alarms before ultimately delivering by a C-section. Each time Joyce would go to the hospital, Edna would broadcast to the worksite, "Ronnie, you better get up here and get in your truck. Joyce is at the hospital!" Many of the workmen heard the announcement, and others heard from the people who had received this message. This happened three times.

My office had the only window that overlooked the parking lot. After a few weeks I began to notice a routine of Edna's. Every Tuesday around ten o'clock she would come into my office, lean over my desk, and stare out the window. I finally got enough courage to ask her what was so interesting. "Tuesdays are when Bub has to come to the courthouse and pay child support to his ex-wife. I was just checking to see if he made it," Edna told me emphatically. Bub was her boyfriend; they never married.

Edna went to work as a field office manager for Foster and

Creighton Paving as soon as she graduated from high school in Gadsden, Alabama. She moved from city to city, following the paving jobs. The last paving job was on I-65 north of Nashville. When that job finished, Foster and Creighton assigned her to the First American project. This was the first time Paul Krambeek had worked with her.

One day, Paul looked out my window and saw some of the laborers working on Edna's car. This was during work hours. He immediately asked Edna what was happening. "There is something wrong with my brakes, and I told Hooten to get them fixed." After further heated questioning, Edna explained that this was routine with the paving division. She said that the men on the job took care of her car and whatever else she needed.

There was no mistaking Paul's reaction. "This is not the paving division! Stop it now, and don't let it happen again!" I was cowering in a far corner, silent, being field trained in human relations. It did not happen again.

Our daughter, Susan Lorene, was born September 17, 1971. She, unfortunately, had colic for six weeks after her birth. I tried to quiet her at night so that an exhausted Joyce could get some sleep. During one of those long nights, I used my "estimating skills" to predict how many Pampers we would have to buy from K-Mart if she continued to soil them at the rate that she was going. She became allergic to the material in the Pampers and we had to switch to cloth diapers. There was no maternity leave, paid or unpaid, for the fathers at that time. She developed into a delightful toddler and kept a smile on my face.

Our rental agreement for our house on Meadowlawn Drive had just crossed the one-year mark. We decided to approach the owner, Mr. Ross Giles, about buying the house. He offered to sell it to us for $12,500. Several of our friends and relatives thought that was too much since it was built for $6,800, including the lot, in 1952. We bought it anyway since the house payments were less than the $100-a-month rent we were paying. The house had radiant heat in the ceiling and no air conditioning. We bought a used window AC unit from the next-door neighbor and were in business. This house sold for $372,000 in 2019. We lived there until 1974.

I grew up hunting and fishing with my brother Ray. This continued in the seventies. I built a dog pen in the back of our lot and got two beagle puppies from Mr. L.I. Mills. These were to become my rabbit dogs. The male pup was Sam; the female, Susie. I trained them until they were able to track rabbits. There was an open field behind our lot that stretched back to the railroad tracks. Our property was buffered from those tracks by a line of small trees and brush that also marked the end of Meadowlawn Drive. Several nights a week I would let the dogs out to hunt rabbits. The baying from their throats when they were tracking rabbits was music to my ears! I hope my neighbors enjoyed the same music.

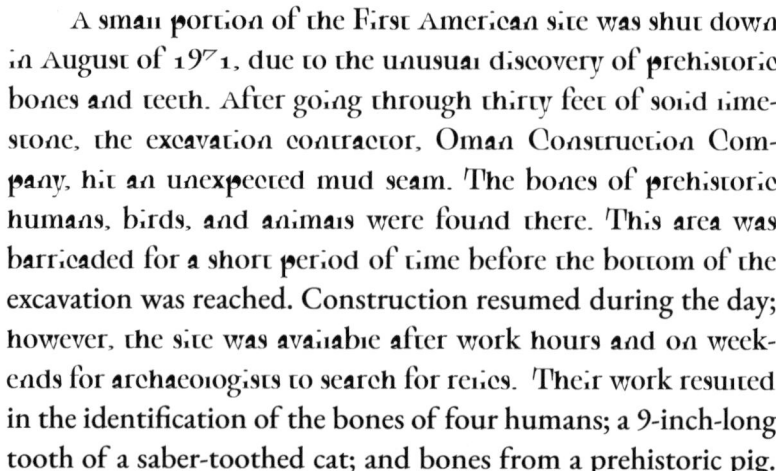

A small portion of the First American site was shut down in August of 1971, due to the unusual discovery of prehistoric bones and teeth. After going through thirty feet of solid limestone, the excavation contractor, Oman Construction Company, hit an unexpected mud seam. The bones of prehistoric humans, birds, and animals were found there. This area was barricaded for a short period of time before the bottom of the excavation was reached. Construction resumed during the day; however, the site was available after work hours and on weekends for archaeologists to search for relics. Their work resulted in the identification of the bones of four humans; a 9-inch-long tooth of a saber-toothed cat; and bones from a prehistoric pig.

The archaeological dig continued several months until it was time to place the concrete slab in the lower level of the parking garage. A manhole was constructed with a traffic cover and a steel ladder that led into the cave. This allowed the dig to continue. The manhole is still there and the saber tooth is on display at Bridgestone Arena, home of the Nashville Predators NHL hockey team.

It is believed that the mud was in a limestone cave that ran to the Cumberland River. In times of low water level, the animals and humans would enter the cave from the river entrance. They died in the cave, possibly by drowning. Over the centuries the mud from the river floods filled the cave, creating the mud seam that was discovered.

A major accident occurred at the First American site that could have affected the future of the Crutcher family. The crane that was used to erect the steel was a Manitowoc heavy duty mobile crane that had a fixed tower. One afternoon I was walking inside the eight-foot-high barricade for the building at Deadrick Street beside the ironworkers' trailer. Suddenly, I heard a loud pop. The crane was approximately 125 feet to my rear inside the barricade and 325 feet from the closest gate of the barricade. I looked up at the crane tower about the moment the ironworkers came flying out of their trailer. They knew what was happening; I did not. The crane was falling!

The steel cables used to lift the loads had become worn and were being replaced. The method to do so was to weld the new cable to the old and pull the cable through the boom onto the cable reel. It was thought that the weld connection became hung in the boom. The crane operator continued to pull when he should have stopped. This caused the boom to collapse and fall back over the cab. The operator jumped to the ground and was not injured. I stood watching when I should have been running like the ironworkers. We were standing about 200 feet to the closest gate leading out of the barricades. Had the crane fallen forward instead of backward, the ironworkers and I could have been seriously injured or, possibly, killed.

The exact cause of the accident was never determined. Before the insurance investigators and federal OSHA (Occupational Safety and Health Administration) could finish the investigation, the only person who knew what happened, the crane operator, died. He and his wife got into a fight, resulting in her killing him.

I stayed on the project until First American Bank occupied their portion of the building and approximately fifty percent of the rental office space had been leased and built out. My next assignment was a job at Ford Glass Plant. I was promoted to superintendent and project manager.

Ford Glass Plant was a large facility in West Nashville. This plant manufactured automotive glass for Ford vehicles. Foster and Creighton Company was one of a select group of union contractors invited to submit bids for construction work at the facility. The work was a modification to the existing buildings.

The project was to remove an entire second-floor slab in one building. This was being done to allow room for a new manufacturing process. My ability to solve problems came into play. The existing floor was composed of 5 ½ inches of concrete on metal decking. There was a large, heavy-duty elevator at one end of the building, which we could use. The first attempt to break concrete into small pieces failed. I had Oman Construction bring one of their drop-hammer machines. It not only broke the concrete, but it caused the metal deck to fall to the floor below. Time for plan B.

Plan B was to rent a large air compressor and six paving breakers from Oman and have laborers break the concrete. The concrete was loaded into two-wheeled concrete buggies, rolled to the elevators, and finally carried to open-top dumpsters. For their safety the laborers were required to wear dust masks and steel foot guards.

There were twelve laborers in the crew. The lead man was James Patterson, a long-time Foster and Creighton employee. The rest of the crew was hired from the union labor hall. I would place an order for laborers in the afternoon for the next day. They would show up at 7:00 a.m., and many would quit at the 9:00 a.m. water break because the work was so strenuous. All were men with the exception of one woman. She did last two days.

I knew James from the First American job. He was a professional laborer and took pride in his work. He got offended if anyone else was operating a paving breaker. James was placed on the center breaker. The job would start each day with all the men in line. By mid-morning the line looked like a flight of Canadian geese with James being the leader.

We started the job by sawing through the 5 ½-inch concrete slab where the floor removal started. Rather than use carborundum blades that wore quickly, I bought a steel blade that had minute diamonds embedded in it. On the first day of the job, James and I put the expensive blade on the saw and tightened the nut on the shaft. I then went back to the job trailer. About forty-five minutes later I heard a light tap on the door. It was James with a long look on his face. He said, "Mr. Ronnie, you better come look. There are a lot of little diamonds all over the floor."

I went with him and discovered that the blade had come off the saw and only five feet of floor had been cut. My question to James was, "It took you forty-five minutes to cut five feet?"

"No. Mr. Ronnie it took me thirty minutes to get up the courage to come and tell you. You can fire me for the expensive

119

blade coming off," was James's answer.

"I am not going to do that. I helped you put the blade on. If I fired you, then I would have to fire myself. We will use the carborundum blades."

One day I saw several Ford workmen hosing down a piece of hot metal that was about 12 x 2 x 1 foot. Surrounding the men were four Ford security guards carrying shotguns. Curiosity was getting the best of me, so I asked James to go see what was happening. James came back in about fifteen minutes. "Mr. Ronnie, the men with the guns said if we could knock off a chunk of that stuff, we would never have to work again. That's titanium, and it's worth more than gold," was James's report. The titanium bar was used as a weir in the furnace to screed the molten glass. When the bars became worn, they were replaced. The old ones were cooled and sold for scrap.

James became more than a Foster and Creighton employee to me. He became a friend whom I counted on to help, for pay, do odd jobs around our house. When we moved from Meadowlawn Drive, he was a vital part of the move. Joyce remembers James lifting a large swing set by himself and carrying it to the moving truck. James unintentionally gave me my favorite nickname, "Mr. Ronnie". He worked for several of my friends on the weekends and used the nickname. It stuck and is used to this day by my closest friends.

———————————————

Our second daughter, Elizabeth MacMillan, was born on January 26, 1973. Joyce had another difficult pregnancy with morning sickness and an appendectomy. However, this time we knew a C-section would be required, so it was scheduled for a Friday. I was outside the nursery with a good friend, Don Savage, when the nurses brought Elizabeth in for clean-up. The nurse held her up for a proud father to view through the window. She was beautiful even with a little nick on her head. I figured it was from the doctor's scalpel.

The Crutchers lived on Meadowlawn until 1974. We were outgrowing the two-bedroom house and were made aware of a house for sale on Lewisburg Avenue. We bought it and got James Patterson and Joyce's brother, Kenneth, to help us move.

The house was built in 1927 by Mr. Thomas McCall, who owned McCall Electric. We were the third owners. It had a detached garage packed with all kinds of records and memorabilia. I don't think the owners before us even went to the packed garage. It was a treasure hunter's dream. I found an original 1910 Boy Scout manual, which I gave to Johnny Green, an original Mickey Mouse watch, and a rare pocketknife.

The lot was very narrow but long. It went from Lewisburg Avenue to the railroad tracks near the Harpeth River. The house and garage were on the front of the lot. The rear had been allowed to grow up in bushes, small trees, and vines. It was impossible to walk or crawl to the railroad tracks. (I tried.) In order to get the lot cleared, I borrowed Joyce's father's tractor and bushhog. I had to back into the "jungle". I eventually got it cleared. I built our daughters an A-frame playhouse on the cleared land.

In 1972, Tim Croft came to Franklin to be the minister of First Presbyterian Church where we were members. Tim and his wife, Carol, had a son and daughter the same ages as our two girls. All our children loved to play together, and our families became close friends.

During this time, Franklin had a problem with pigeons roosting on the Presbyterian and Methodist churches at Five Points and Little Mills grain silos and the Masonic Hall on First and Second Avenues. The Franklin Fire Department would periodically organize a "pigeon shoot". Word would go out to select Franklin residents, and the shoot would occur in early morning. I was a "select" because our next-door neighbor on Meadowlawn was a fireman. The "hunters" would divide into groups and go to the four locations. There could be as many as forty or fifty shooters, each with a semi-automatic shotgun. The noise was deafening!

Since I had taught Tim to rabbit and dove hunt, I invited him to the shoots. After all, pigeons roosting in the First Presbyterian Church attic was a problem and he was the minister. Tim would be in a group near the grain elevators. I would stay near the churches. It was a grand time shooting for the thirty minutes. I continued to participate until I looked down the barrel of my shotgun, sighting a pigeon, and saw the stained-glass window of the Church. I was in a split second of shooting the window! I didn't shoot. After I stopped shaking, I put my gun in my truck. I never participated in another pigeon shoot.

Friday night was adult night for the Crutchers and Crofts. We got babysitters and went out on the town. Tim had a personal rule not to do anything on Saturday night except to put the finishing touches on his sermon for Sunday. He left Franklin in 1976 and went on to serve churches in Virginia, Florida, and North Carolina. We remained friends until Tim's death in 2018. Carol died in 1984. We stay in touch with their children and his second wife, Margaret.

We were happy with the house on Lewisburg Avenue but began to long for a newer home in a subdivision. Johnny Green, acting as our real estate agent, found us a house in the Monticello

122

subdivision, just north of Franklin off Hillsboro Road. We moved there in 1976. There were a number of children in the neighborhood who Susan and Elizabeth played with. They still remember the good times they had on Halloween.

After finishing the Ford Glass project my next job was on the Vanderbilt University campus. Foster and Creighton Company was selected by Vanderbilt to convert Neely Auditorium from a conventional fixed stage with fixed pews to an experimental performing arts theater. Neely had been built by Foster and Creighton in 1925. I was assigned as the project manager and superintendent. As a student I had attended chapel services and Western civilization history classes in Neely. The work started with the demolition of the entire interior of the building, including a massive pipe organ.

The pipe organ had a blower driven by an electrical motor. After our electrical subcontractor, Travis Electric, disconnected the electricity to the building and removed the panels, I directed Pappy Choate, a laborer, to take a hacksaw and cut the one-and-a-half-inch copper cable to the motor. As soon as he cut through the insulation, the saw exploded! Pappy was not hurt. The only damage was to the blade of the saw. It was burned and destroyed. The motor had been fed by high-voltage electricity from the building next door, Alumni Hall, by an underground cable. The cable, nor the disconnect, were on any of Vanderbilt's drawings.

My favorite hobby—junk and salvage—was born at Neely. The pews were given to a church. The Gothic-style chandeliers were sold to a laborer, who resold them at a good profit. The green slate floor became part of an architect's contemporary house built on top of Sneed Hill in Williamson County. I bought the circa 1925 plantation fans and resold them. These were the days before reproductions could be bought. Much to Joyce's chagrin, junk and salvage is still my primary hobby.

Foster and Creighton Company was later awarded a separate Vanderbilt project to upgrade Alumni Lawn, located in front of Neely Auditorium. The carpenters and laborers taught me two things that were not in my engineering textbooks. The architect, Mr. Bob Street, wanted new sidewalks with edges that were curvy, not straight. I was preparing to spend time measuring from the architectural drawing and stake the curves. My carpenter foreman, Phil Burns, stopped me and said, "You don't have to do that, watch."

He filled a hose pipe with water, capped both ends, and laid out the walk. I then called Mr. Street to come and approve the layout. After adjusting the hose pipe 'snake', he approved the layout and thanked us for making it so fast and easy. We staked down the hose and used it to guide the carpenters in forming the sidewalk.

The second lesson learned occurred after the walks were finished. Dr. Alexander Heard, chancellor of Vanderbilt University, used the walks to go to Rand Hall, the dining hall, for his morning coffee. He complained to the Department of Campus Planning that the walks looked too new and needed to be darker. The university's engineer, Charlie Mitchell, directed me to estimate the cost to replace the offending walk with one using brown cement and river gravel. We suggested that, over time, wet leaves would stain the walk. However, we were told the Chancellor wanted them "old" now. I gave Charlie the estimate for a new walk but continued to try to darken what we had. We tried using wet leaves with limited success. My laborer foreman,

124

Bobbie Hooten, stepped up and said, "Strong coffee will do the trick."

Early the next morning, before the path was being used, we made several pots of coffee and spread it on the walk. When Charlie saw it, he was happy. Dr. Heard must have been happy, because he never complained again.

After the Neely project, the company was selected to renovate and expand a house in Belle Meade, off campus, for Vanderbilt University President Emmett Fields' residence. I was the superintendent and project manager for the expansion.

In March 1978, there was a major controversy in Nashville over Vanderbilt hosting a Davis Cup tennis match between the United States and South Africa. The concern was that by doing so it would say to the world that Vanderbilt didn't care about the injustices associated with the apartheid government in South Africa. Protestors for and against the match gathered on campus around Memorial Gymnasium. There were threats to the top administrators at VU. Campus planning asked all the contractors working for Vanderbilt, on campus and off, to man their jobs while the matches were being played.

One match was to take place on a Saturday afternoon in March. I found myself giving up a fishing trip that Saturday and sitting on a new backhoe in President Fields' yard. There were armed security guards onsite. They wanted us, myself and a laborer, to be as obvious as possible from the street, so we wore bright yellow safety vests. Our tasks for the day were to remove a tree and its roots and start digging footings.

I learned to operate the new backhoe while looking over my shoulder for cars driving by with guns or dynamite. Fortunately, all was quiet and peaceful. I stayed on that job until I went to Saudi Arabia with Foster and Creighton International.

125

11

TURN AT THE EUCALYPTUS TREE

1978 – 1979

FOSTER AND CREIGHTON Company had formed a wholly-owned subsidiary, Foster Creighton International (FCI), to do work in Saudi Arabia. This company was chartered in the Grand Cayman Island to take advantage of the different Internal Revenue Service Rules for offshore companies. Wilbur Creighton III, owner of FCI, hired a new staff to fill all positions. Preference went to employees of Foster and Creighton Company to fill any job for which they were qualified. FCI had been awarded a $28 million contract to undertake a major expansion of the powerhouse and electrical system to the King Faisal Specialist Hospital.

I had heard of the high salaries being paid for working in Saudi Arabia, so I went to interview with Gerry Guy, vice president of Mid-East operations. After a short interview he offered me the job as general superintendent. I would be working onsite at the King Faisal Specialist Hospital in Riyadh, Saudi Arabia. The position was a promotion; the problem was the salary offered was too low. His offer was only ten percent over what I was earning. I said, "Thanks, but no thanks."

Paul Krambeck, who had been promoted to assistant vice president of operations, told me to come into his office.

"How did the interview go?" he asked.

"Good, I would like the job Gerry offered, but the salary was too low." I told Paul what he offered.

"Let me talk to Wilbur tomorrow," was Paul's comment.

Gerry Guy asked me to meet with him the following afternoon. The meeting was short and sweet. He increased my salary offer by fifty percent. Paul had done his homework and found out what the new hires were to be paid. Also, he had spoken with Wilbur III.

Prior to my interviews, Joyce and I discussed the opportunity. I explained to her that while living in Saudi Arabia she would have some strict cultural regulations, meaning she would not be allowed to drive and her clothing, though loose fitting, must cover her entire body from head to toe. I also told her that the variety of food would be limited, household water would be delivered by truck, and she should not expect to see any grass, only sand and dirt. I went on to say that I would be working six days a week.

"Is it going to be that bad?" was her question.

I answered, "I don't know. This is what I have heard. I will sign a contract for eighteen months. There will be a ten percent bonus if I complete my contract. If we decide to go, I plan to collect my bonus."

"I'm in, but we need to discuss this with the girls before we make a firm decision," Joyce said.

We had a family meeting and the girls were excited about

going to live in a new country. We told them that they would be able to finish preschool and first grade in the States. We went on to explain that Dad would go in April and they would follow in June. This was in the spring of 1978.

The trip to Riyadh was quite an adventure. The contract that Foster and Creighton International signed required that the job be manned in a short period of time; so, all the company personnel who were going were sent to "man the job". Tu Bourland went in February for the initial set up of the villas and offices. The remaining personnel who transferred to the international company went in April. Those in this group were Frank Blair, with his wife Florence; Scotty Goodrich, with his wife Brent; Tom Pirtle, and me.

The trip started out with problems. Our visas to get into Saudi Arabia were being processed in the Saudi embassy in Washington, D.C. and had not arrived in Nashville by the time our flight to New York was to leave. We were told to go ahead and fly from Nashville, with the promise that the visas would be waiting for us at John F. Kennedy Airport.

We had a four-hour layover in New York before the flight to London. Wilbur Creighton had given us his pass to the American Airlines VIP lounge. This is where we spent the four hours, with good food and drink. We were also anxiously awaiting our visas. The visas finally arrived an hour before we were to depart.

The rest of the trip was long, boring, and uneventful until we arrived at the Riyadh Airport around ten o'clock at night. We cleared customs with no problems. My paperback copy of the New Testament made it through inspection even though Bibles were banned from Saudi Arabia.

We had been told by Gerry Guy that someone would be in the airport lobby holding up a sign saying "FCI". We were to go to that man, and we would be carried to our villas. We looked for the man with the sign. No man with an FCI sign was to be seen in the crowded lobby. We were concerned, to say the least. We had no money for a phone call or taxis, no addresses for our villas, and none of us spoke Arabic. We finally got a guard to call the phone number we had for Ti. No answer. Sometime after midnight, Ti walked into the lobby! There had been misinformation about our arrival time.

Although the vice president of Mid-East operations, i.e. Gerry Guy, was yet to arrive, we went to work immediately. Ti and Frank organized the main office downtown, while I worked with Scotty and Tom to set up the field office at the hospital worksite. We met the plant manager for King Faisal Specialist Hospital (KFSH), Bob Harper. Bob was British and lived in Riyadh with his wife Mavis. He was responsible for the entire physical plant and wanted all construction work to run smoothly. He gave us (FCI) the use of several block buildings for jobsite offices. He remained helpful throughout the project.

The construction sites were fenced with metal roofing panels nailed to wooden 2x4-foot stringers. These horizontal stringers were supported by wooden 4x4-foot posts set two feet in the ground. The panels flopped in the wind, nails were missing, and posts were leaning. These were very sloppy sites, and we knew we could do better.

We worked with local laborers (most from Yemen) to build a better fence. String lines were pulled to assure a straight fence. The 4x4 wooden posts were set and concrete filled the holes. Nails were driven eighteen inches on center (o.c.) to secure the panels to the stringers. We were proud of our work until the first sandstorm came. It hit during the day, but it was so strong that the thick sand blocked out the sun. We were huddled in the field office, expecting the roof to be blown away at any second. The storm lasted no more than ten minutes, and the roof held.

The first thing we saw when we stepped outside was that our sturdy fence was still in one piece, but lying flat on the ground. The fence would not let the wind pass through. It built up so much force that the posts were broken at ground level. We had learned our lesson. The fence was rebuilt with half the nails and no concrete in the post holes. Our new fence flapped in the breeze as did every other sloppy fence in Riyadh. The locals had a good laugh at our expense!

FCI leased a tract of land near the KFSH and hired a contractor to build the workers' camp. One hundred workers from Thailand were hired and imported. They were of various trades, i.e. carpenters, equipment operators, pipe fitters, sheet metal mechanics, and cooks for the Thai camp. They were skilled, hard workers, who had been trained at trade schools in Thailand. Each worker was issued a numbered brass disc. This disc was used to check-out hand tools and log-in with the payroll clerk. About five of the men could speak English and they became foremen. None of us could speak Thai.

One Friday, which is the Holy Day for the Moslem faith, I was at the jobsite catching up on paperwork. Friday was the one day of the week that no one worked, so I was alone. Around nine that morning, there was a light knock on the office door. It was the Thai general foreman. He shouted, "Mr. Singh, Mr. Singh, we can't find Mr. Singh!"

"Calm down, who is Mr. Singh?" I asked.

"Number 10! Number 10, like on the brass tag!" was the answer.

"When was the last time anyone saw Mr. Singh?" I asked.

"About midnight, we were at Lord's camp for a party. When we got back to our camp, no Mr. Singh," said the foreman. Lord was another contractor with a Thai camp.

"Were you drinking raisin wine?" I questioned, trying to get the fun story.

131

"Not me, but maybe Mr. Singh," he answered.

Raisin wine is an alcoholic drink made by fermenting raisins. It, as with all alcohol, was and still is illegal in Saudi Arabia. The imported workers were required to stay in their camps when not working. Knowing all of this, I took the foreman to visit the closest Saudi jail. We were not allowed in the jail but could see some of the prisoners through the window bars. No Mr. Singh!

It was time for me to get some help. Til Bourland was in charge of the Thais and the camp. I went to his villa and got him out of bed. I explained the problem and had him take over. I went back to the jobsite office; Til went to find our Saudi liaison and the foreman went back to the Thai camp. We were to gather at my office in one hour. The plan was to tour all of the jails until we found Mr. Singh. At the end of the hour, we were all gathered except for the foreman.

He arrived at my office later saying, "We have found Mr. Singh; he is at the camp."

Mr. Singh had more than his share of the raisin wine and had gotten homesick for Thailand. He started walking across the desert to his homeland. After some time, he got sleepy and laid down in the sand for a nap. The next morning the hot sun awakened him, and he wandered back to the FCI Thai Camp.

Joyce, Susan, and Elizabeth came to Riyadh in June, of 1978. Their route was through JFK Airport in New York City and London's Heathrow Airport, before arriving in Riyadh. The trip started smoothly in Nashville, but hit a snag at JFK. They had boarded their plane and were sitting on the runway awaiting take-off when they were informed there would be a delay. Their flight was scheduled to leave at six that evening but did not get in the air until midnight. They had planned to eat dinner on the plane; however, they were told that they could not be served until they were airborne. The girls begged for food and milk but were given none. Joyce had her hands full trying to entertain hungry and thirsty girls in a hot, stuffy plane.

I had flown from Riyadh to London to meet them and escort them to Saudi Arabia. Custom clearance could be a problem for an unescorted woman with two small daughters. I had arrived the day before their flight and enjoyed the break from the dust and alcohol ban. I had a good dinner at my hotel in Trafalgar Square and took in a movie. I was pleasantly surprised that drinks were served in the theater.

I had planned to meet my family the next day and take them with me on a short sightseeing excursion of London before we all boarded the plane to Riyadh. I checked out of the hotel and went to Heathrow Airport where I learned the flight from JFK had been delayed six hours. I forgot about sightseeing anything except the airport.

When my family did arrive, it was a welcome sight for my eyes. Susan and Elizabeth were wearing new matching outfits. Both girls had new, shorter haircuts. A lifelong memory is seeing the girls rushing to me and us hugging.

The delay from JFK made the flight connection to Riyadh tight. We rushed to the Saudia airline terminal, arriving just in time to board. Joyce was exhausted. The six-and-a-half-hour flight from London to Riyadh was uneventful. Joyce was interested in the designer clothes the Saudi women on board wore at the beginning of the flight and how they changed into the veils and burqas as we neared Saudi Arabia. We cleared customs and went to my station wagon to go to our villa. It was after 1:00 a.m. when we got to bed.

For breakfast that morning we had cold cereal and milk. That was all I had been able to purchase. Joyce and the girls would be picked up later that day by one of our two Yemeni

133

drivers and carried grocery shopping at the stores and souks. Shopping was a half day excursion. One had to travel to various shops and souks (open air markets) to find all of the food and staples needed. Local fresh meat and poultry were avoided. The meat we cooked was bought frozen from a distributor that delivered to the U.S. Corp of Engineers' compound. No pork was allowed in Saudi Arabia; instead, we had turkey sausage and turkey bacon. The women didn't mind how long it took to shop since there were not many other things they were allowed to do.

Our drinking water came from KFSH. The hospital had its own state-of-the-art water treatment plant. The plant treated the salty, brackish water pumped from the deep aquifer of Saudi Arabia. This water was not fit for human consumption without being treated. We were allowed to carry two five-gallon plastic jerry cans to our villas each day.

The water used for our bathrooms and clothes washing had to be bought from vendors driving tank trucks. They would dump it into an underground cistern. From there the water was pumped to a water tank on the roof of the villa where we lived. (This was a standard practice in Riyadh.) Gravity created enough pressure to flush the commodes, take a shower, wash clothes, etc. One did not drink this water.

The play area for Susan and Elizabeth was on the flat, paved roof of our villa, which was enclosed by a four-foot parapet wall around the roof. Joyce had bought an inflatable wading pool for the girls, and we placed it on the roof and filled it with water the day after they arrived. After letting the girls play in the pool, we left it on the roof with water still in it.

When Joyce and the girls went back to the roof the next afternoon, there was no pool. After I got home that evening, we talked about what could have happened. Our first thought was that the pool had been stolen. We quickly ruled that out, because no outsiders had been in the locked building. Too, the roof was approximately 50 feet in the air and there were no roofs adjacent to our villa that were that high. We concluded that, due to the low humidity and 110-degree temperature, the water had evaporated; the wind had blown the pool off our roof. I even drove around the neighborhood looking for the pool but without any success.

Living conditions greatly improved two months later when FCI rented a larger, nicer villa and a shipment of furniture arrived from the States. The two-story villa had four apartments, all occupied by couples working for FCI. Inside the surrounding eight-foot high privacy wall was a nice in-ground swimming pool. The furniture shipped from Nashville was top-of-the-line from Davis Cabinet Company, including beds, chest of drawers, and dining room tables. Life was good!

In addition to our family, the families occupying the other three apartments were Scotty and Brent Goodrich, Antone and Aida Arnouk, and Jerry and Lena Heasley and their daughter Tessie. There was a small outbuilding within the villa walls where Rosey, the Somali maid, lived. She worked one day a week in each apartment.

The villa was the gathering place on Friday for many of the FCI personnel. Joyce made delicious homemade hotdog and hamburger buns (neither were available in Saudi) that were shared with all the families. Others brought more food, and a good time was had by everyone. The swimming pool adjacent to our apartment was also a popular Friday activity for the families. The pool was clean, thanks to Joyce. But the water was always cold. Even though the outside temperature was over 100 degrees Fahrenheit, the low 10-15% humidity and the circulating water led to rapid evaporation, meaning the water never got warm.

One Friday morning as we were eating breakfast, we looked

outside our back door and saw a baboon walking around the top of our villa wall. To the delight of the girls, we tried to catch it. We were not successful in our attempts and it disappeared. The next morning a Saudi neighbor tried to stop Scotty Goodrich's truck as he headed to the KFSH jobsite. Scotty did not stop. That evening the Saudi followed Scotty to the villa. Outside the villa gate was a very upset Saudi. Our Syrian liaison person, Antoine, who we called Uncle, came from his apartment and met with the neighbor. After a heated discussion the neighbor went away.

Uncle came into the villa laughing and told us that the Saudi was complaining that our pet baboon had chased his sheep and eaten his bananas. He demanded that we come and catch the baboon and pay for the damage. If we did not, he would kill the animal. Uncle told him that it was not our pet and that it had just appeared the previous day. Furthermore, Uncle told the man he didn't need our permission to kill it. We never knew what happened to the baboon.

FCI furnished the pick-up trucks that were made available to the mechanical subcontractor during the project. All our vehicles were maintained by a Somali mechanic, McDoo. The trucks had powerful engines and were capable of high speeds. Two of the mechanical foremen had to go to Dhahran to get some critical equipment. The road to Dhahran was a two-lane, straight stretch, but it followed the topography, i.e. a lot of hills. Late in the day, the foreman had the truck running wide open about the time he topped a hill and saw a group of Saudis butchering a camel in his path. The animal had been hit and killed and the remains were still in the middle of the highway.

The Saudis first heard the truck and did not react. But when they saw it speeding toward them, they jumped off the roadway. The foreman could not stop in time to avoid the camel carcass.

When he and his co-worker were able to stop and check the damage to the truck, they found that the exhaust system had been torn off and a good bit of the camel was lodged in the truck underbody. They continued to Dhahran, got their equipment the next day, and returned to Riyadh. By the time the truck was delivered to McDoo it was ripe! It took a lot of talking and a few extra riyals (Saudi currency) to get him to fix the damaged truck.

There was an independent school in Riyadh which had been started several years earlier by the U.S. Corp of Engineers to educate the children of their employees. It was open to any child in kindergarten through ninth grade who was non-Muslim. We were fortunate in that our company would pay the tuition so Susan and Elizabeth could attend the school.

Elizabeth would be entering kindergarten. On her first day, she was met by Mrs. Mary Munin Rice Whitey, a Franklin native whose mother had brought the monkey to my fifth-grade class. *"It's a small world after all... it's a small, small world ..."* Mrs. Whitey was a teacher at the school. Elizabeth, however, was in Mrs. Maureen White's class; she was from Canada. Susan was going to be in the second grade. Mrs. Angela Mayhew, who was from Australia, was her teacher. Soon after Susan started the school year, she started speaking with a British accent. We loved hearing her talk.

Joyce, who has a degree from George Peabody College for Teachers, wanted to teach at the International School. She applied for a position and got an appointment for an interview with the superintendent. He was a professional educator from Arkansas.

Joyce prepared for the interview by arranging her school records and letters of recommendation. She entered the superintendent's office expecting a long interview and the superintendent saying that he would look over her material and get back to her. She was shocked when she told him that she graduated from Peabody and he said, "I don't need to see anything."

"Why?" Joyce asked.

His reply was, "Peabody College is the best teachers' college in the United States, so I am going to hire you without looking at your resumé." He then told her that she would be teaching eighth and ninth grade math and science. She walked out of his office with a big smile on her face.

Our project required a new hydraulic elevator. FCI had a contract with Schindler Ltd. (UK) to furnish and install it. The normal construction procedure is for the general contractor (FCI) to build the elevator shaft and then turn it over to the elevator subcontractor. The subcontractor would mount the permanent guide rails. A drilling rig would be mounted on the rails and used to drill the shaft for the piston. (The piston is the permanent part of the elevator that raises and lowers the elevator cab). That is the accepted practice used in the States.

I was walking through a KFSH construction site next door to ours, which was being built by Pepper Construction, based in Chicago, and observed an unusual sight. There was a tripod set up that was being used to lower and raise buckets of dirt and rock. Upon closer examination, I saw that a four-foot square vertical shaft was being dug. In the shaft was a small Thai worker with an electric chipping hammer and a light. Another worker used the tripod to pull the buckets of rock chips. I found the jobsite superintendent and asked him what was happening.

"We are mining for a shaft to install the piston for an elevator," he said.

I replied, "We have an elevator in our project. We're counting on our elevator sub, Schindler, to drill the shaft from the guide rails."

"Schindler is our sub also. They excluded the drilling from

138

their contract, because they don't have their drilling equipment in Saudi Arabia," was his comment.

I immediately went back to our field office and called our purchasing agent, Al Johnson, and asked him if Schindler had excluded the drilling from our contract. After checking, he said, "Yes."

If we drilled a shaft for the piston before the floor slabs and roof were completed, we could use a standard well-drilling rig. Al Johnson and Tim Bourland went looking for well drillers and found several. At this point, I called Gerry Guy and told him he needed to make a deal with a driller and get him to drill as soon as possible. An agreement was made with a driller, but it did not include the water needed to keep the drill hole wet. We weren't concerned, thinking that what little water was needed could be gotten from the faucets in the powerhouse. We were wrong!

The drilling had gone down less than ten feet before the bit hit rock fissures and small seams. The drill water disappeared immediately. We needed truckloads of water, not just a few gallons. The driller was preparing to pull off the job if we didn't get the water to his rig. I called Gerry Guy and told him he needed to negotiate with the well driller. He and Fahon, the FCI interpreter, came quickly. I told him to do whatever necessary to keep the rig on the job. The drilling continued; we bought truck after truckload of water to dump in the hole. Still, the drilling was stopped constantly while they awaited the delivery of more water. The driller charged for his downtime.

We may have spent as much (or more) money than Pepper did, but we did it safer and quicker. The hand mining could have resulted in some men getting killed by the earth collapsing; moreover, it probably would have taken two months. The Saudi Government had good safety laws modeled after our OSHA (Occupational Safety and Health Authority). If they inspected

139

the site, they would have issued a stop-work order and fined or arrested someone.

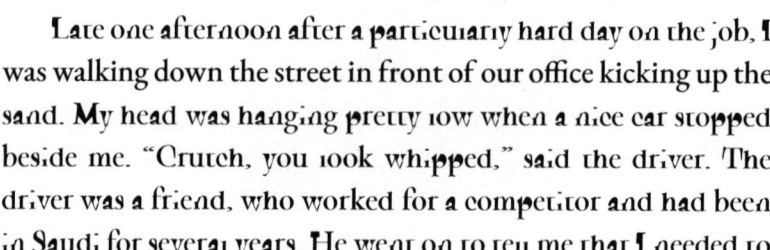

Late one afternoon after a particularly hard day on the job, I was walking down the street in front of our office kicking up the sand. My head was hanging pretty low when a nice car stopped beside me. "Crutch, you look whipped," said the driver. The driver was a friend, who worked for a competitor and had been in Saudi for several years. He went on to tell me that I needed to get my mind right.

"There are four classes here–Saudi citizens, Muslims from other countries, Westerners, and then others. If you expect equality for all, you will go crazy," was his advice. I got my mind right. I realized I was a second-class citizen. I was a visitor in this country, and I spoke only one language.

In August of 1978, our family was riding in our station wagon going to have dinner with some friends at their villa. We rode past a Yemeni camp on the way. It was dusk. The sun had set. The camp was occupied by Yemeni laborers and their families living in salvaged cardboard boxes. Just as we got next to the camp, we heard a loud, ear-bursting explosion and smelled burnt gun powder. Dust immediately filled the air making it difficult to see the roadway. I thought that the Yemeni were making illegal bombs using dynamite, and that one accidentally exploded. I didn't want to be there when the Saudi police arrived so I "put the pedal to the metal" and did not stop until I got to the friends' house. I later learned that Ramadan, the holy month for Muslims, began that day. It begins when the new moon is observed and is announced by the firing of a cannon. The cannon happened to be sitting beside the highway just as we passed!

After six months with FCI, I was due a vacation with the family. Bangkok, Thailand was the destination selected. We flew from Riyadh to Bahrain on Saudia Airlines and changed to Singapore Airlines for the flight to Bangkok.

Bangkok was fascinating. The first thing that caught my eye, as a builder, was the use of 6-inch diameter bamboo poles lashed together to make scaffolding for work on the exterior of five and six-story buildings. We saw this on the way to The Intercontinental Hotel where we stayed.

We checked into the hotel about noon and went to the restaurant there. The food was great and was of such a variety that each one of us was able to get exactly what we wanted. The fruits and vegetables were fresh, and the dessert bar was extensive. But we were warned not to drink the tap water in our rooms for fear of infectious bacteria.

One day we took a riverboat cruise up the Chao Phraya River. It was a guided tour with a smaller boat taking us up some tributaries. We saw people living in stilt houses over the water. One family would be throwing their wastewater in the river while in the next house someone would be brushing their teeth with the river water. Very enlightening!

At one stop there was a man with a 10-foot Boa constrictor snake. For a fee of a few Baht ('Thai currency') one could have their picture taken with the snake wrapped around them. The girls wanted their picture taken, so money changed hands. I took the picture since Joyce would not get within fifteen feet of the snake. Another good time!

The Thai National Independence Day occurred the week we were in Bangkok. The Intercontinental had an elaborate outdoor show with a buffet for adult hotel guests that night. Joyce and I hired one of the hotel maids to babysit Susan and Elizabeth so we could attend the party. The show was very good, and

141

the food was even better.

We went back to our room after the show. The girls were in bed, and we paid the maid. We had a big drink of water from the water pitcher before going to bed. Early the next morning, both of us awoke with stomach aches. We thought we had food poisoning from the buffet the night before. But the girls, who were not sick, said that they drank all the water from the pitcher while we were gone. The babysitter, they told us, had refilled it with water from the sink faucet. We quickly recovered from our brief illness and made sure we had a new pitcher filled with water that was safe to drink.

Shopping at a large mall was a treat. It was better than the two malls in Nashville—Green Hills and One Hundred Oaks. We bought clothes and souvenirs. I got several safari suits (the rage of the Mideast) and an elephant carved from mahogany wood. Joyce purchased Thai silk. Susan and Elizabeth picked out Thai dolls. We also purchased a doll for my stepmother's doll collection. We bought a woven chest in which we put our purchases so they could go on the airplane back to Riyadh.

After spending a week in Thailand, we headed to Riyadh. First, we flew to Bahrain, where we were to change planes to fly Saudia Airlines to Dharan. We arrived around 10:00 a.m., and our connecting flight was to leave at 11:00 a.m. When we got to the terminal, the message board said our flight had been delayed. We were stuck in Bahrain. We checked every thirty minutes, but could not get the departure time to Dharan, where we would connect to our flight to Riyadh. Finally, around three o'clock in the afternoon, I asked if our flight to Riyadh had been rebooked. The attendant answered,

"Oh, you want to go to Riyadh?"

My obvious answer was, "Yes."

"Oh, we have a direct flight to Riyadh leaving in thirty minutes. Come out on the runway and show us which bags are yours, and we will load them on the plane to Riyadh."

Our contract for the KFSH expansion required us to build the massive pads for the four General Electric 'GE' generators that KFSH had purchased. These were to be powered by natural gas turbines. They would create the 60-cycle electricity for the hospital. This was to replace the 50-cycle system installed by the British during the original construction. Each of our pads had eight, 2-inch diameter bolts. These were to be used by the installers of the generators to anchor them to the pads.

Scotty Goodrich and Jerry Heasley used the latest surveying instruments to assure the anchor bolts were set according to the GE shop drawings. We knew they were set right. The installation contractor hired by GE was Irish. A crew of Irishmen came in and immediately tried to disprove the anchor bolt layout.

The base plates that were to go over the bolts had 4-inch diameter holes. This allowed 1-inch play on each side in the setting. We argued for some time, set up surveying instruments, and pulled string lines. It was obvious the Irishmen were wanting us to pay a change order for them to modify the bolts. This occurred on a Thursday. On Friday, the Irishmen drank too much of some Irish beer they had smuggled in with their tools. Saturday morning their heads were hurting and they were red-eyed, but they were on the jobsite. We started banging the base plates and anchor bolts, hoping to align them to suit the Irishmen. After holding their heads for thirty minutes, they decided the anchor bolts were okay and proceeded to install the generators.

Fridays became our Sabbath days. Although Christian church services were forbidden by the Saudi Government, they were held in various Western compounds as long as they were not advertised and no crosses were visible outside the building. We occasionally attended a church service in the SANG 'Saudi Arabia National Guard' compound. The Americans living in the compound were pilots there to train Saudi pilots. The church had two services, one for Arabic-speaking Christians and one for English-speaking Christians. Joyce had brought Sunday school books and used them to teach the girls.

Fridays were also our day to explore Saudi Arabia. We expatriates would share directions to points of interest. A popular trip was to a petrified forest outside Riyadh. The directions were simple but hard to believe. "Go to the end of the street 'which was paved'. Travel eight kilometers north. Turn east at the eucalyptus tree. Go five kilometers to the forest."

With a lot of doubt, we left with water and snacks. Sure enough, after driving about eight kilometers we saw a lone tree on the horizon. It was the only tree there and it was a eucalyptus! After turning east and driving five kilometers we were in the forest of sticks and limbs. It was sobering to stand in the desert and realize that these limbs and sticks had been there since prehistoric times.

We took an all-day trip one Friday with Antoine and Aida Arnouk. Our destination was a large oasis. On the way, we encountered an elaborate equestrian complex. Antione wanted to stop and visit. Since he and Aida spoke Arabic, we pulled in the drive. Antoine talked with one of the gate guards and learned that these were the stables for a Saudi prince's racehorses. We were asked to leave and we did.

Another interesting sight on the way to the oasis was a dairy farm where a herd of Holstein milk cows were kept in a bare, fenced-in field. They had to be fed hay or feed, because there was no grass for grazing. I remembered that I had seen some beautiful alfalfa hay being raised in irrigated fields. Now I knew where it was going–to the cows. Limitations in agriculture meant strict regulations when it came to farming. For example, the Saudi Government subsidized processed flour so the Saudi citizens could afford it for bread. Some Saudi dairy farmers bought the bags of flour and fed it to their cows. The bags of flour were cheaper than the hay. They were caught; the Saudi Government put a stop to the practice.

The oasis was like those you read about in *The Arabian Nights*. Water came up from the ground and flowed down a gentle stream for about a kilometer before disappearing into the ground. Saudi Arabia is situated over a massive aquifer that erupts in various fissures in the rock. There were groves of date palms and other trees. Small areas were separated by live hedges of vegetation for privacy. The areas had manicured grass lawns. Arab families gathered at these grass plots to picnic. The women and girls had their bodies covered with their burqa 'full body covering'. We saw several families roasting lambs. The young boys played soccer, the universal sport. These Friday excursions taught us about the native culture.

A part of the King Faisal Specialist Hospital powerhouse expansion was the installation of a new steam boiler. This was a large, heavy piece of equipment that had to be set on a concrete pad. The pad was 150 feet from the outside wall of the hospital. The boiler had to be lifted from the bed of the transport truck by a crane and swung to the pad. There was a large Manitoba crane parked on the KFSH campus when we arrived at the job-site. It had been left by a contractor who had been asked to leave the country.

Bob Harper, the KFSH plant manager, was responsible for ensuring the crane was properly maintained. I asked him if we could rent it to set the boiler. I told him that Jerry Hensley was a qualified crane operator. Bob said, "Part of my job is to see that this crane will run and move, so you will be helping me if you use it at no cost."

Jerry checked the crane, got it started, and drove it to our job site. The driver of the transport truck carrying the boiler parked near the crane. Word had gotten out about what was about to happen, and a crowd gathered. This occurred in the early after-noon, the hottest time of the day. The steel cable slings of the crane were attached to the boiler, and Jerry slowly lifted it from the truck bed. He then started the 180-degree swing toward the concrete pad. As it neared the pad, Jerry had to set it down about 30 feet short of the pad.

"The cables are slipping because of the heat. We will try again early tomorrow while it is still cool," Jerry told me and the crowd of onlookers who had gathered to witness what was an unusual event to locals.

We planned to try again at seven the next morning. When I arrived at 6:30 a.m., I was shocked at what I saw. The boiler had been successfully set on the pad.

"Jerry, what went on? The cables must not have slipped," I said.

Jerry's answer was, "Slipping cables was not the problem. There was not enough counterweight to keep the crane from tipping over. I asked the concrete contractor to bring his bull-dozer over and place its' blade on the crane's counterweight. The increased weight of the dozer was enough to keep the crane from tipping. We did this an hour ago, before the crowd arrived."

Jerry parked the crane back in its original slot. Bob Harper was happy that it had been utilized and continued to be in full working order.

———◦———

Christmas 1978 was not the best in our marriage. In fact, there had been only one worse—Christmas 1968 when I was in Vietnam. FCI had rented a cargo container in which our families in the States could ship Christmas presents to us. When it arrived in Saudi Arabia, it was opened and inspected by Saudi customs' agents for contraband, then shut and turned over to FCI. On what would have been an otherwise happy day, those of us picking up our shipments swung the container's doors open and were furious by what we saw. The presents sent by our families had been ripped open and the name tags were gone. We had a list of the presents and were able to get most of them delivered to the right people. But we also had to tell our families that some items were missing, and, to top it all, we had some items that did not belong to anyone in our company. It was more than frustrating.

Our major gifts to Susan and Elizabeth that Christmas were bicycles we bought at the souks, but they had to be assembled. Scotty, Til, and Tom helped me late into the night put the bikes together. These bikes would be ridden on the villa roof, not in the street. There were no sidewalks. After the ordeal that year, I promised Joyce that we would be in Franklin for Christmas 1979.

In June of 1979, our family went for a visit back to the States. We flew non-stop from Dhahran, Saudi Arabia to New York on a Pan American 747-SP. The plane was less than fifty

147

percent full; we were in the air for fourteen hours. The girls slept lying on the seats (with the armrests folded up). Thankfully, the food was delicious and plentiful.

Our flight arrived in New York early in the morning. Our flight to Nashville didn't leave until 1:00 p.m., so we had time to see one sight. We chose the Statue of Liberty. After the rough roads and crazy driving in Riyadh, we were looking forward to a smooth ride in a clean Yellow Cab. We were disappointed. We got an old Plymouth with worn-out shock absorbers. Joyce and the girls sat in the back seat and had their bottoms bumped every time we hit a crack in the road. We took the ferry to the monument, had a quick tour, and headed back to the airport. We picked out a new Marathon Yellow Cab for the return trip.

As we drove south on I-65 after leaving the Nashville airport, we were amazed at the green trees and high, green grass in the median. We spent a week just being with family and friends and eating Mrs. McMillan's good food. We then went to Miami, Florida to visit our friends, the Crofts. From Miami I returned to Riyadh via Frankfurt, Germany. Joyce, Susan, and Elizabeth returned to Franklin to spend a few more days.

On their return trip to Riyadh, they stopped in Athens, Greece for a few days of sightseeing with me. I flew from Riyadh to meet them. We stayed in Glyfada, a southern suburb of Athens. We toured the Parthenon and the sights around it. It was particularly interesting to me since Foster and Creighton Company built the full-sized replica of the Parthenon in 1922 in Nashville. We went to the National Museum and saw fabulous paintings and sculptures. The hotel where we were staying had all the fresh popcorn we could eat, to the delight of the girls. We also took a day-long cruise to some of the small islands and villages along the coast of Greece. We saw how the villagers lived, and we swam in the blue Aegean Sea.

The airline bringing Joyce and the girls to Athens lost one of Joyce's bags which contained a new blender. We checked daily to see if it had been found. It showed up minutes before we boarded our flight to Riyadh.

In Saudi, traffic accidents were commonplace. By Saudi law the blame for the accidents was split amongst the participants on a percentage basis. If a Westerner was involved, he ('women weren't allowed to drive') got a share of the blame based on the rationale that if he had not come to Saudi Arabia, the accident would not have happened.

The FCI group had a few minor accidents. One of our American summer workers, the son of an FCI executive, rear-ended a local citizen and abandoned our truck by taking a taxi to the jobsite. We called Uncle. He came out and called the police. He negotiated with the police and the other driver on the spot. Riyals changed hands, and the matter was settled.

One of our superintendents had a Saudi driver cut in front of him causing a minor fender bender. The superintendent refused to accept the fine proposed by the police and, instead, took the citation to appear in court. A few days later he went to court. He was accompanied by Uncle and Fahon, FCI's liaison and a Saudi citizen. A Saudi citizen was required to advocate in all legal matters. Fahon pleaded the case, stating that the superintendent's truck was at a dead stop at the time of the accident. He went on to say that the other driver had tried to get in front of the superintendent, which was how he hit the FCI truck. The judge found the superintendent guilty and FCI paid the fine.

The Crutcher family had one close call, but it did not involve the police. The four of us were going downtown in my station

149

wagon one Friday. Joyce had taken off her head scarf to get some relief from the heat. She had also pulled her full-length dress to her knees attempting to cool off a bit. As I was driving, a large Mercedes Benz dump truck, traveling in the lane next to us, got too close and peeled the rubber protective strip from my front bumper. I quickly pulled away from him and shouted about his recklessness and not paying attention to the road. Joyce, who could look up and see him, replied, "He was paying attention to my exposed chest and legs, not the road." We kept our minds right!

A new concrete cooling tower was in the scope of our contract with the KFSH. A cooling tower is used to take out the heat picked up in the chilled water circulated throughout a facility. The one we built had a three-story concrete shell. Inside the shell were clay tiles stacked on top of one another. The tiles had open webs that allowed the water to cascade down from the top to a basin at ground level. The tiles were hand-stacked. The workmen did not get all of the packing material out of the tower before water was turned on. The basin filled with water and pieces of packing material, card board, wood scraps, and metal strapping material. This trash had to be removed.

The cooling tower contractor who we hired had his Turkish workers remove the debris. Several of the men stripped to their underwear and jumped in the basin. The water was about five feet deep and was quite turbulent. It took less than an hour to clean out the trash but the men wanted us to leave the water flowing. They didn't want to come out of the cold water. I went to their boss and asked why they wanted to stay in the water. He laughed and answered, "They are living in tents in the dusty desert and get a shower only once a week. This is the only bath they have had since leaving Turkey."

In early November, 1979, Joyce reminded me that I had

promised her the year before that we would not spend another Christmas in Saudi Arabia. I said, "You are right. Tomorrow, I will request FCI to get the visas and tickets."

Around 6:30 a.m. November 21, 1979, I was driving by the airport listening to BBC radio. We received uncensored news on the BBC, but our reception was only good at night and in the early morning. The announcer said that there was some kind of uprising in Mecca, Saudi Arabia, but details were sketchy. As I drove, I passed the airport and noticed that planes were taking off. I was not concerned about the uprising, because the Saudis immediately shut down airports when a crisis occurred. If the planes were flying, the uprising must be minor. I continued driving to the jobsite. It was a normal workday.

That night Joyce's mother telephoned us. To receive a call from the States was extremely rare and not even possible without the assistance of FCI. What we did not know was that FCI stateside had arranged for the employees' families to call, so they could be assured we were okay. The media in the States were reporting the seriousness of the uprising in Mecca.

When Mrs. McMillan telephoned, she wanted to know if we were okay, making the comment "Those people are crazy!"

While we were talking to her, a strange voice interrupted us, screaming "You can't say that, you can't say that!" It was a Saudi censor. Our conversation was abruptly ended by the censor.

The uprising was serious. The Mosque in Mecca was seized by two hundred armed civilians, calling for the overthrow of the House of Saud. They took over Masjid al-Haram (The Great Mosque). The planes that I had seen flying the day of the uprising were actually ferrying Saudi Arabia National Guard (SANG) troops to Mecca and bringing the wounded back to Riyadh. This continued for two or three weeks until, with the help of the French, the Saudis overcame the uprising. In all, 127

151

civilians and soldiers were killed; 451 were wounded; and 67 rebels captured. On January 9, 1980, weeks after we were safely back in the States, 63 of the rebels were beheaded on the public squares of the major cities in Saudi Arabia.

We packed our bags and left Saudia Arabia in early December. We were thankful that we had our tickets and visas. I was asked to come back to Riyadh after the New Year for a couple of months to help finish the job at KFSH. I told FCI's Paul Briscoe, who was in charge, that I would if it worked out with my future employment with Foster and Creighton Company.

On our way home we stopped in London for a few days. Harrod's Department Store was the favorite attraction. Susan and Elizabeth sat on the lap of Father Christmas and had their pictures taken with him. We were also fortunate to see the Changing of the Guard at Buckingham Palace and the Tower of London where the the Crown Jewels are secured.

When we landed in New York, an airline stewardess started a conversation with us. We told her that we had been living in Saudi Arabia. She said, "Welcome to the good ole USA!"

Soon after we had gotten home, I went to meet with Roy Slaymaker to discuss my future with Foster and Creighton Company. I told him that FCI had asked me to come back to the KFSH project for two or three months. Roy was not a supporter of Foster and Creighton International, and he let it be known in his reply.

"Vanderbilt 'University' has selected 'Foster and Creighton' to make a major renovation to the football stadium," he told me. "I was counting on putting you in charge. The project will start in May."

"Could I go back to Riyadh until March since the architect

will not have the 'Stadium' plans ready before April?" I asked.

"No, you make up your mind. Either come back to Foster and Creighton now or go back to Riyadh. If you choose to go back, I will select someone else for the Stadium," Roy said.

I made the decision immediately.

"I'll take the Stadium project," I said without hesitation.

Prehistoric relics unearthed during the excavation for the new bank prompted archaeological research on the site. (Courtesy Les Leverett)

First American Bank Center construction site, 1971. (Courtesy TSLA)

Once the archaeological site was established all interested parties allowed the creation of a permanent access point so future research could take place underground. (Courtesy Tennessee Division of Archaeology, Nashville/Aaron Deter-Wolf)

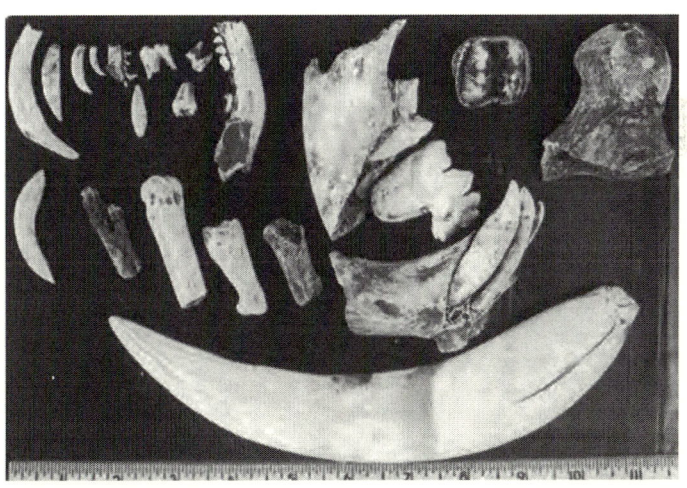

The remnants of another age paused our project and became the subject of future expansion of Nashville's identity, especially with the naming of The Predators professional hockey team. (Courtesy Les Leverett)

155

Upon its completion, First American Bank Center became a central focus of downtown Nashville's late-century economic development identity.
(Courtesy TSLA archives)

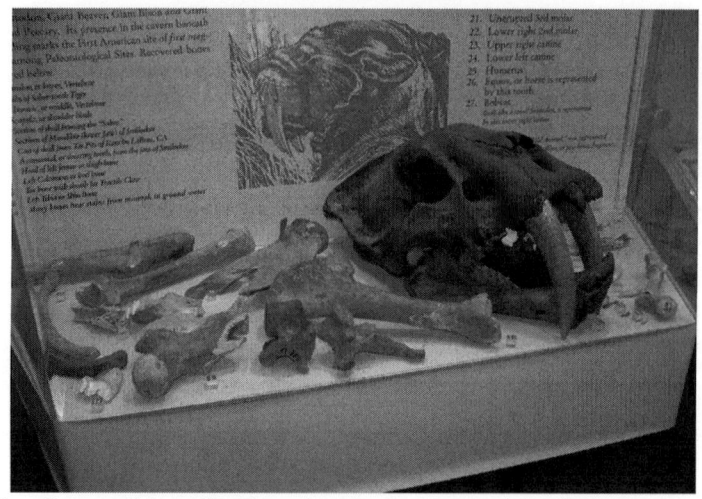

The collection of the archaeological remnants was on exhibit for many years in the First American Bank building in downtown Nashville.
(Courtesy Tennessee Division of Archaeology, Nashville)

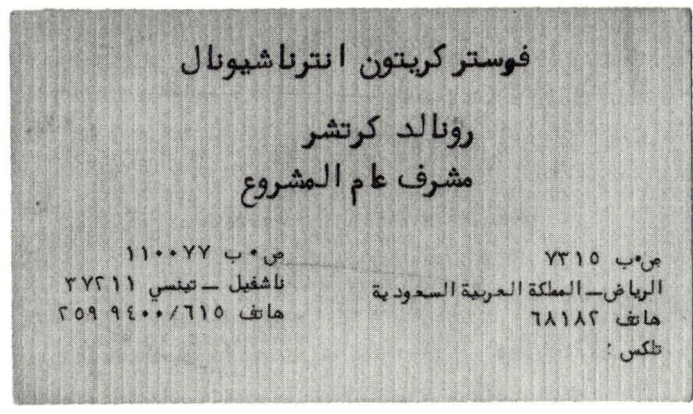

Foster and Creighton Company has a rich heritage in Tennessee and the Southeast. In addition to numerous sites, the replica of The Parthenon is a legacy of its own.

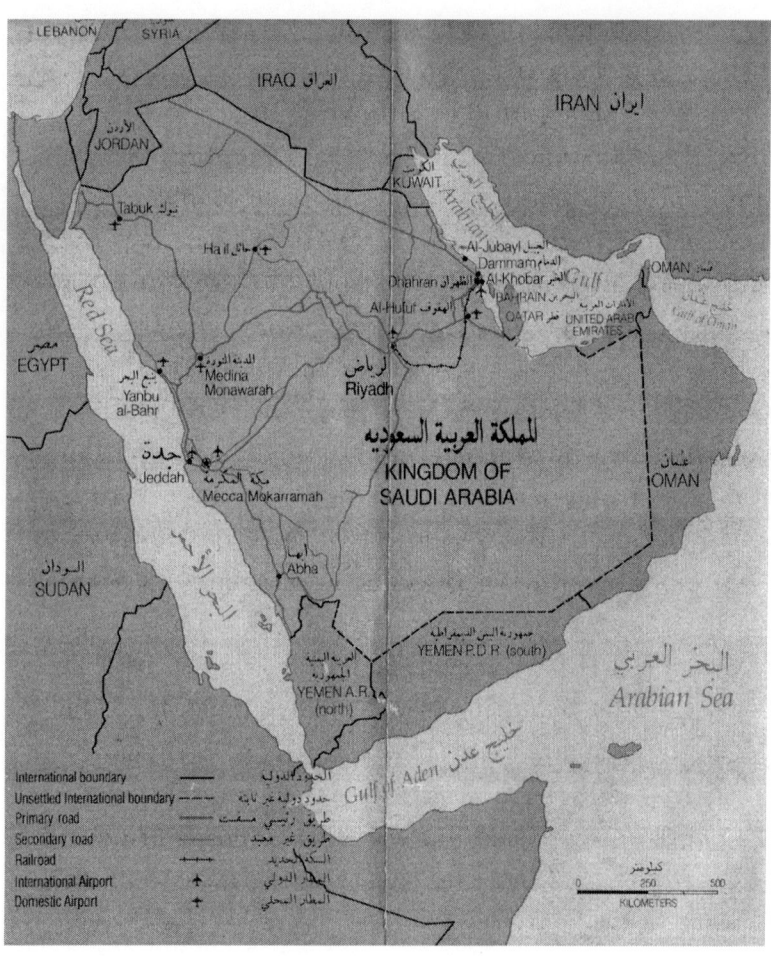

Moving to Riyadh, Saudi Arabia to work on the King Faisal Specialist Hospital for Foster and Creighton International was a pivotal point in my career.

GRESHAM, LINDSEY, REID, LTD.

*Our task was to construct the expansion of the hospital. The climate, the
culture, and the vast difference in work procedures taught me a great deal about
adaptation. (Courtesy Foster and Creighton Collection Nashville
Metropolitan archives)*

*Beyond the two large boilers in the foreground, the cooling tower
construction, which was challenging, is shown in this photo. The desert horizon is
faintly recognizable. (Courtesy Foster and Creighton Collection,
Nashville Metropolitan archives)*

Elizabeth, left, and Susan are ready for their new school in Riyadh, 1978.

There really was a eucalyptus tree!

I took Joyce, Elizabeth, left, and Susan on many interesting outings in Saudi Arabia, but we always looked forward to returning to the "good Ole USA."

LAYING CORNERSTONES

12

Back to the good ole usa

1980 – 1982

I HAD ALWAYS BEEN ABLE to talk honestly with Roy Slaymaker. He was a straight shooter. My experiences in Saudi Arabia were solid examples that illustrated that I could lead and be trusted in an operational setting, one that also fit the roles required for executive leadership. At my request, we discussed my long-range future at Foster and Creighton Company. I made a direct inquiry of Roy. I did not mince words.

"How long will it be before I can expect to be promoted to assistant vice president?"

Roy replied, "The latest vice president, who was just promoted, was hired two years before you. If things go well, you could be assistant vice president in 1984."

This promotion would be a significant event in my career. With the increased responsibility came the opportunity to purchase stock in the company, in addition to associated benefits

165

that were appearing. I was promoted in 1984, just before Foster and Creighton Company ceased operations.

The renovation of the Vanderbilt Stadium, also traditionally known as Dudley Field, was my only Foster and Creighton project in 1980. I began preparing for the renovation from my office at Thompson Lane. In May 1980, we opened the field office and I moved onsite. The project had a deadline of September 12, 1981, not an insignificant date. This was the Saturday that Vanderbilt would play its first game of the football season, also a home game.

The project had a very synchronized timetable. We could work onsite at the Stadium through the summer of 1980. But in September, we had to halt any construction, so that Vanderbilt could play their football games in the Stadium. It was going to be extremely challenging, but after some of the situations I had encountered in Saudi Arabia, I felt comfortable.

During that summer of 1980, several things happened so the deadline could be met. The artificial turf field was replaced. (It was covered with tarpaulins after the '80 football season to protect it from construction dust.) The spectator bench seating on the steel portion of the stadium was removed. After the steel was sandblasted and painted, new aluminum planks were installed.

While this was taking place at the site, work was beginning to start off site. Breeko Industries was casting the precast beams and seat risers that would replace all the existing concrete in the Stadium. The timetable for this project was somewhat complicated. All onsite work had to stop from September 20 to November 30 for the collegiate football season. Then, we had a total of 212 work days to complete the massive renovation because Vanderbilt would play its first game of the 1981 football season in the Stadium.

The original Vanderbilt football stadium was built in 1923.

It consisted of a concrete horseshoe-shaped structure. Not surprisingly, the concrete had deteriorated and was becoming unsafe. Levy Wrecking Company had the contract to remove the steel-framed press box and the concrete. As soon as enough concrete was removed, the drilling rigs moved in to drill for the piers. These went down to rock to support the new structure.

Once the piers were in place, concrete columns were cast. These columns supported the precast beams that had been fabricated by Breeko. These beams were transported to the site and erected. This was followed, shortly thereafter, by the placing of the seating slabs.

While this concrete work was proceeding, the structural steel contractor was preparing to raise the steel portion of the Stadium by ten feet. (No small job.) First, steel columns were tied together with temporary beams, then 28 hydraulic jacks were positioned to raise the entire west side of the stadium. This process took fourteen hours, six of which was to repair a beam that collapsed. Once the west side was raised, new columns were placed on the original footings and welded to the bottoms of the original columns. This procedure was repeated on the east side.

A new three-level, steel-framed pressbox was built on the west side. The first level had ten viewing booths set aside for VIP visitors who the Chancellor would invite; among this group would be major financial donors to Vanderbilt. The next level was for the press—print journalists and radio reporters. The top level was used by the television crews. Redwood 2 x 4s, salvaged from the original bench seating, were used to build TV camera platforms. This was the only salvaged material that was repurposed.

As soon as the steel seating was raised, the existing patron areas, including the bathroom facilities and toilet stalls, as well as concession stands, were demolished. They were replaced with newly designed ones to meet the Stadium capacity determined by the Metro Codes Department.

Vanderbilt University Athletic Director Roy Kramer was the driving force behind the entire renovation and expansion. He worked closely with the architects from Walk Jones and Francis Mah, Inc. and the engineers representing Michael Baker, Inc. to develop plans that suited the needs of his Vanderbilt football program, the Davidson County Metropolitan Codes Department, and the University's budget.

Mr. Kramer took an active role in the design, particularly how it affected the football program operations on game day. For example, he wanted the new concession stands designed to accommodate the greatest amount of countertop space possible. He had a formula that forecast concession sales based on the number of linear feet of countertops. The initial plans had plastic laminate, or Formica, tops. But during freezing weather the laminate will come unglued from the plywood underneath. Due to the expense, marble tops were out of the question. The lead architect, Mike Feinstein, had seen countertops made of smooth concrete at the Liberty Bowl in Memphis. The decision was made to use concrete countertops.

The tops needed to have sharply cut edges rounded out for safety. We located a shop in Nashville that could bend sheets of steel. These bent sheets became the forms for the tops. After making a sample top and getting Mr. Kramer's approval for it, we went into production on site. We used the extra concrete left in the truck after a day's placement elsewhere in the Stadium. Under other circumstances, this concrete would have been wasted. After the concrete tops cured, they were coated with two coats of sealer. These concrete counters are still being used.

Sadly, we had one man killed on this project. An ironworker

was installing the bolts in a low beam which was about fifteen feet above the concrete floor of the concourse. He had his hard hat and safety harness on; however, he had disconnected the harness lanyard so that he could walk from one end of the beam to the other. When he was halfway across, he lost his footing and fell to the concrete below. His head was severely injured. He died in the hospital a few hours later.

In the afternoon the following day, I was working late when I heard a knock on the jobsite office door. It was the family of the deceased man. They were wanting to see where he had been injured. I escorted them to the Stadium near the site of his fall, but moved away while they mourned as a family. This was a sobering moment for me.

This project crew included two women who were working in the field. One was a carpenter accompanying the crew installing the aluminum bench seats. On her first day, she came with her carpenter's toolbox filled with tools resting on her shoulder. She stood just under five feet and weighed around a hundred pounds. The men didn't expect her to last, but she performed well. The second lady was an electrician with a robust build that was suited for construction work. Her assignment was to use a mechanical device to bend four-inch steel conduit pipe into 90-degree sweeps. Each sweep weighed over forty pounds. She first used a Greenlee bender to form the sweeps and then carried them on her shoulder to locations throughout the stadium for installation. The men said they did not like to work with her, because she didn't use a cart to move the pipes like they did.

When the last seating was being installed, an off-site dispute arose between the owners of the company erecting the aluminum seats and their field superintendent, a man named Dick. The two company owners drove to Nashville from Detroit in a fancy new Cadillac to pick up some of the tools and equipment that Dick was using. They arrived after Dick and his crew had quit for the day. Dick had secured his portable electrical generator to the painted steel handrails with a chain and padlock. The owners didn't have a key to the lock, so they tried to beat the lock open with a piece of scrap steel. They had taken their suit coats off and loosened their ties. They were banging away when they looked up and saw a menacing sight. Staring down at them was Huey, the ironworking superintendent. He wore a large hardhat, had a full red beard, and was carrying a large wrench.

"Can we help you?" one of the owners asked Huey.

"Maybe," he replied. "Mr. Crutcher tells me that you are trying to take Dick's generator and I am to stay out of it. I don't know who owns the generator, chain and padlock, but I own the newly painted handrail that the chain goes around. If I see one scratch on the handrail, I will come looking for you."

The owners got their leather driving gloves from the Cadillac and placed them under the lock before resuming the pounding. They weren't successful in getting the padlock removed.

The Vanderbilt Stadium renovations and expansion were completed Friday, September 11, 1981. The following day Vanderbilt beat the University of Maryland 23-17.

For this opening game, Vanderbilt gave all the construction workers and their families free tickets in one section of the end zone. A football from a field goal kick went into that section. When the ushers came to retrieve the football, none was to be found. Supposedly, one of the workmen let the air from the ball, put it under his shirt, and went home with a souvenir.

13

EXCAVATIONS, DEMOLITIONS
AND OBSOLETION

1982 – 198₅

IN 1982, NASHVILLE, under the leadership of Mayor Richard Fulton, was considering building a hotel/convention center. There were competing groups hoping to be named builder for the future center. One group approached me about being project manager if they and their site were chosen. Their site was near Charlotte Avenue and Twelfth Avenue North, where the new Amazon Operations Center is now being built. It was an informal interview. I told them that if they were successful, I would consider their offer. I did not feel it necessary to tell Roy Slaymaker that I had been approached.

As it turned out, Foster and Creighton Company got the contract to build the Nashville Convention Center 'NCC' on a different site, the city block bound by Broadway, Fifth Avenue, Commerce Street and Sixth Avenue. This was to become my

171

next major project.

Besides me, the project staff consisted of Edna Newton, an administrative professional, and our field engineer, Roy Jackson. We set up a field office in an existing building at the corner of Seventh Avenue and Commerce Street. The project site required no excavation at Fifth and Broadway, but solid limestone with a depth of 40 feet had to be removed along Commerce Street. While the architects representing the firm Yearwood, Johnson and Crabtree were designing the convention center structure, we contracted for the excavation. Approximately 250,000-cubic yards (1700 dump truck loads) of rock had to be blasted, excavated, and hauled away.

The NCC was a part of an overall plan to revitalize downtown Nashville in the eighties. This plan involved boring underneath the downtown streets to install steam and chilled water lines from the Nashville Thermal Transfer Plant to the convention center and other buildings. It also involved widening Commerce Street from Fourth Avenue to Eighth Avenue.

Roy Slaymaker and I met biweekly with the architects at the offices of Metropolitan Development and Housing Administration (MDHA) to review the overall progress and collaborate on design issues. In one such meeting the architects noted that they had encountered a design problem when trying to make the NCC main entrance handicap accessible. The existing Commerce Street elevation was lower than the proposed design for the entrance. One solution would be to lower the NCC main floor to match Commerce Street. This would not work because the ceiling heights underneath would be reduced. Roy Slaymaker solved the problem.

"Commerce Street is being redesigned; so, why can't it be raised so that it is level with the entrance to the NCC?" Roy asked during our meeting. "The limestone chips from the

172

tunnel boring machines can be used as fill to raise the street."

This was a brilliant solution. I learned a lot about creative thinking from Roy that time and on other occasions. The changes were made to the Commerce Street plans. A credit against the original bid was then obtained from the boring contractor, since he didn't have to haul the chips away.

One block of Sixth Avenue had been officially abandoned when we started the project. All of the utility companies had removed their lines except Nashville Electric Service (NES). They had several street lights along the abandoned portion of Sixth Avenue. Power had been disconnected, but the poles and lights remained. I had contacted NES several times to get them to remove their poles. The answer I always received was, "The work order is in, but it's not high on our priority list."

As the excavation contractor was moving his drill rigs to Sixth Avenue, I called NES again. I reached the dispatcher and explained that the lights had to be removed.

"We only send out a crew if there is an emergency, like a pole leaning in a traffic lane. Is this an emergency?" the dispatcher asked.

"Not now, but it will be tomorrow when the contractor blows up the street and the lights and poles fall," I replied, adding, "Do I need to wait until the street is dynamited and call in an emergency?"

"No, no! We will have a crew there tomorrow morning," he promised. They were there at 7:00 a.m. the next day.

Excavation was finished. All the rock had been hauled to BNA Airport, where it was used to build a new runway. The architectural plans were now completed. We were now ready to bid the project.

Metro ran into difficulty selling the bonds needed to proceed with construction. My team had to shut the field office down and move back to Foster and Creighton's main office on Thompson Lane. During the shutdown, enough water accumulated in the excavated hole for wild ducks to land there and take up residence.

The Creighton family decided to get out of the construction business in 1983. It was rumored that they had an interested buyer from the West Coast, and the company was apparently more attractive to the buyer as an on-going business. After checking the assets and doing some due diligence, the opportunity was suddenly not as appealing. The buyer had learned that the investment would require a much larger loan than would have been feasible. Without that buyer, the Creighton's decided it was time to liquidate.

On Sunday, February 12, 1984, I received a call from Roy Slaymaker as I was preparing to go to church. He asked me to come to his house for a meeting. When I arrived, I was greeted by Roy and three company project managers—Til Bourland, Tom Pirtle, and Jim Brownlee. His opening statement set the tone for our meeting.

"Wilbur 'Creighton' is shutting the Company down Tuesday."

He went on to say, "I am forming a new company, and I want you to be part of it."

Til was the first to speak. "Roy, that takes a lot of money, and we don't have it."

Roy then told us that he had two longtime friends who would back us, and money was not a problem. For years, they had encouraged Roy to start his own company, but he remained loyal to Foster and Creighton.

The friends were Bill and Clark Akers, brothers whom Roy had known from childhood. The Akers had been successful at contracting, coal mining, and asphalt paving. They had retired in 1981 at which time they formed a company to manage their assets for their children. They named their firm The Parent Company LLC.

The four of us told Roy we would be a part of his company. The Akers gave us a fair deal, making us minor shareholders and giving us an opportunity to buy their shares after five years. The Akers let us use the name The Parent Company, Inc. ("TPC"). They transferred the general contractor's license they held over to us. The Parent Company, Inc. was hired to finish all of Foster and Creighton's work in Middle Tennessee, and we even hired some of the former F&C employees to work for us. We chose not to sign with the unions. We offered our workmen better benefits than the unions.

The Akers were instrumental in creating a profit-sharing plan for TPC; every employee received a bonus if a profit was made in the fiscal year. That bonus was based on a percentage of the employee's salary. The percentage was the same for all employees, regardless of their position.

We set up our first office space in a separate wing of the F&C Building on Thompson Lane. After a few months, we moved to offices in the BNA Center near Nashville's airport. We moved again in 1991 to Powell Place located in the Maryland Farms Office Park of Brentwood. A few years later in 1996, The Parent Company purchased a house and lot on Wilson Pike Circle, also in Brentwood. We demolished the house and built a 10,670-square-foot office building. This is the present home of TPC.

As soon as we formed in 1984, we began cultivating new projects; and we visited many of Foster and Creighton's clients in our first week of business. Vanderbilt University was one of those clients. During the meeting, I remember we told the head of campus planning, John Waterman, that Foster and Creighton Company was no longer in business and we would like to be considered for Vanderbilt projects. Mr. Waterman responded, "If a Creighton walked through that door, I would not recognize him. You are the ones we depend on for good work. We were going to call F&C next week to invite them to come and talk about a new job. You come instead."

We were in business.

In my forty plus years in construction, it was rare that I had to fire someone, much less a whole crew. This happened in 1984. TDC was in the process of completing a Foster and Creighton project, the Brentwood Commons Office Complex Phase II. Versco, the non-union branch of F&C, was the construction company onsite. I was assigned to oversee the completion. After reviewing the status, I went to the jobsite and met with the superintendent. We discussed the fact that the job was several weeks behind schedule and what could be done. He assured me that his crew would finish the project on time.

Weekly progress benchmarks were set, and I checked on the job every other day. The first benchmark was not met. I supplemented his crew with some top-quality men that TDC had retained from F&C. The Versco superintendent was a good, Christian man but was not motivating his crew. I brought in more men, including a superintendent. The more men I added to the job, the slower the workers from the original crew became. In construction terms, they were 'slow walkin' the project. Knowing that this was Versco's last job, they were trying to make it last as long as possible.

176

I showed up at the job around ten o'clock one morning with paychecks for the workers in the original crew. I told them that we didn't need their services any longer. The superintendent handed out the checks, blessed me, and he and his men left the jobsite. One of the workers in the replacement crew that my superintendent brought in had been asking his foreman earlier in the week why he and his crew had to work so hard if the Versco men were being allowed to slack off, or, as they say in the industry—gold brick.

The foreman said to him, "How much is The Parent Company paying you?"

The man told him what he was making to which the foreman replied, "Are you happy with that?"

The worker's answer was, "Yes."

"Then give TPC your hardest work and don't worry about the other fellows," concluded the foreman.

As the fired crew was leaving the jobsite, the foreman went to the questioning worker and said, "Now you know why I told you to earn your pay."

The contract for the Nashville Convention Center was ultimately transferred from Foster and Creighton to The Parent Company; so, we reopened the jobsite office for the Nashville Convention Center in early summer of 1984 with a completely new office staff. The new office manager was Sharon Parsons. Dan Cundiff was the assistant project manager and Buford Wilson was the field engineer. Roy Slaymaker had a desk in our field office and spent twenty-five to fifty percent of his time there, helping with the project management.

The Nashville Convention Center 'NCC' was being built

using an industry standard method called Construction Management. In this method, the construction manager, The Parent Company, separated the total work into trade packages. These packages were individually developed for the work of a single trade, i.e. concrete, steel, plumbing, electrical, etc. Each trade package was bid and the contracts awarded to the low bidder by the project's owner, the city of Nashville through MDHA. The construction manager's responsibility was to coordinate the trade contractors' work to see that it complied with the plans and stayed on schedule. The construction manager was paid a fixed fee. The trade contractors were paid by the project owner.

Construction resumed after the one-year financing delay. We bid and contracted for the various trades. The first trade was the concrete work, responsible for installing foundations for the steel columns and building retaining walls. This was followed by the structural steel erection. The plumbing, electrical, and mechanical contractors began as soon as the concrete work would allow. The construction work proceeded as scheduled without any delays other than a strike by the plumbers' union. It was settled without delaying the total project.

The city of Nashville created a NCC staff to operate the center, which initially included purchasing for materials that the construction industry refers to as FF&E (Fixtures, Furniture, and Equipment). Many members of the staff were new hires from outside Nashville. The task of purchasing so much FF&E was so overwhelming that they were falling behind schedule. The City hired TPC to take over the purchases; we got the procurement back on schedule.

Because the NCC was part of a downtown revitalization project, existing buildings located within the project's domain had to be removed. TPC was hired to oversee the demolition of the legendary Sam Davis Hotel, as well as a smaller building that

178

housed a large print shop. In place of these, TPC would oversee the construction of a new parking garage. We also represented the City in the building of a 27-story hotel connected to the NCC.

The demolition of the Sam Davis Hotel instantly became a media event, especially since it had been a part of the Nashville skyline since 1928. As construction managers, we obtained bids for the demolition and selected the low bidder, Levy Wrecking Company. They chose to use explosives to take down the structure, which meant selecting the least intrusive time possible. The demolition was planned for 7:00 a.m. on Saturday, February 16, 1985.

MDHA, on behalf of the City, was able to utilize the penthouse of the National Life and Accident Insurance Company (NLAIC), a 31-story building located two blocks from the project, as an observation site for the event. (Today, it is a Tennessee government office building, The William R. Snodgrass Tower.) Because it was taller than the Sam Davis, the NL&AIC was an appropriate place to host a viewing party for the implosion of the historic hotel. Invitations were sent to MDHA board members and other dignitaries. TPC furnished the coffee and donuts. I took my younger daughter, Elizabeth, who had just turned twelve. She was offered the opportunity to push the plunger to set off the explosives but declined. A large crowd of about five hundred, spectators and media reporters, had shown up for the event. It was a major part of the local news cycle for a couple of days.

A few months later, Levy received the contract to demolish the large printing shop nearby. They told us the demolition, by explosives, would take place on a Sunday morning. I drove to the site on the Saturday afternoon before to see how preparations were going. I was shocked to find only rubble remained of

179

the print shop. Levy had already blasted. The superintendent decided the project could do without the publicity and crowd that the Sam Davis demolition created.

———————————————

Before the NCC could be opened for business, all the life safety systems had to be tested. One of these was the fire alarm system. A fire hall was located at Second Avenue and Demonbreun Street, five blocks from the NCC. The station fire chief arranged a viewing of the complete test of the fire alarm system. We were invited to join the chief on the twenty-seventh floor of the convention center's hotel, located beside the convention meeting facilities.

The test consisted of (1) a fire alarm being pulled in the NCC, (2) the signal going to the Metropolitan Nashville Fire Department (MNFD) dispatcher, and (3) a hook and ladder crew being dispatched from the station on Second Avenue. The small group of us observing the test from the hotel's top floor could clearly see the station and the route to the convention center. The chief was expecting a good show.

He started the test by radioing one of his men at the convention center to pull a fire alarm. We watched as the doors of the fire station opened and the two-segment hook and ladder truck started to roll onto Second Avenue. The fire chief must have noticed that the engine had left the station without the rear driver because I heard him screaming into the radio for someone to "get on!" His face turned white and the expletives he used don't bear repeating. The rear driver is absolutely necessary for navigation of the long trailer, as it must handle sharp turns. The fire chief knew that without that man the engine could not navigate the 90-degree turn at Demonbreun Street. He was right. The fire engine didn't stop. It ultimately knocked over a streetlight. What was to be a proud display of MNFD readiness turned out to be an embarrassment. Later, a second test was run without an audience. It passed.

The first scheduled show in the Nashville Convention Center was the Nashville Boat Show, which was held in February 1987. The entrance to the exhibition hall was at Broadway and Fifth Avenue. The architects had been instructed to design the entrance to allow a boat to enter that met the interstate highway clearance restrictions. As boats were being transported and guided into the exhibition hall, one rather large participating vessel encountered difficulty.

A tall yacht, which had been transported using an interstate route, became stuck as it was being maneuvered through the entrance. After investigating why this happened, it was discovered that the yacht owners had bought a permit that allowed them to exceed the interstate legal height limit by one foot. There was only one remedy. We had the concrete contractor remove the concrete entrance ramp. The yacht was then able to enter. After the Boat Show closed and the yacht was removed, a new ramp was placed—one with a slope one foot lower than the original.

The financing bonds that were sold in 1984 to pay for the Nashville Convention Center were retired in 2014. Revenue collected from a city hotel-motel tax, rather than property taxes, fulfilled the city's debt obligation for that project. In the 1990s, The Parent Company expanded the convention center to connect it to the new Nashville Arena 'Bridgestone Arena' that was built across Broadway. The convention center meeting facility was demolished in 2017 to make way for what is referred to today as a mixed-use development. The hotel, which was not razed

181

for the project, is being remodeled and incorporated into this new development.

I realized I was old when I began witnessing buildings that I had built become obsolete.

14

BRINGING IN A NEW PERSPECTIVE

1986 – 1997

IN THE MID-1980s, Robert Ring, who had recently been elected Williamson County Executive (now called Williamson County Mayor), wanted an alternative to the traditional low-bidder method of contracting for new public buildings. I became aware of his interest and invited him to visit The Parent Company's work at the NCC while it was still under construction in 1986. He made the trip to Nashville, and we toured the project. I explained in detail how the construction management method was being used. Mr. Ring liked what he saw and heard. Not long after, the county board of commissioners, with his leadership, moved to change the county's process for contracting, developing a construction management approach to the county government's building program.

The first time Williamson County officials adopted this method was during the planning for a new jail complex. Originally

183

located in downtown Franklin, near the Public Square and County Courthouse, the jail facility was inadequate. A decision was made to relocate the Sheriff's office and detention facility to a new site off Columbia Avenue, a couple of miles south. Proposals were submitted by various firms for the construction management contract. The Parent Company was selected. We began work in 1987 with completion in 1989.

Though unrelated to the actual construction project, two personal memories stand out from this experience. The first involves the operation of the cold drink machine. Our girls, teenagers by then, wanted to earn spending money. I wanted them to learn how to operate a business. On most jobsites there is a cold drink vending machine that is leased from a major soda drink supplier, i.e. Pepsi, Coke. Someone at the jobsite is tasked with dealing with the leasing company, which means paying the rent and ordering the drinks. The machine must be stocked and restocked; coins have to be removed, sorted, wrapped in rolls, and deposited in a bank. That "someone" became the Crutcher sisters. They learned that cold weather and rain were not reasons to delay stocking the machine, which was just outside the jobsite office.

Susan and Elizabeth soon realized that the vendor was charging them more for the drinks than they could be bought at Wal Mart (reminiscent of their daddy's experience at BGA). They renegotiated the lease on the machine with the vendor so they could buy and stock it with any brand they chose. Their daddy was proud!

The second incident occurred on a Saturday. In fact, it was Christmas Eve 1988. I left our house in Monticello subdivision and headed south on Hillsboro Road to check on the jail project. The sun was shining; the temperature warm for December. I noticed some small limbs on the roadway but thought nothing about it. On my return home around 10:00 a.m., I heard on the radio that a F4 tornado had touched down in Rebel Meadows, less than a mile from our house. It lifted, then came down southeast of us at Spencer Creek Road and Gray Fox Lane, about a mile from where we lived. It demolished a house belonging to Ernest Rice. Mr. Rice was killed when the roof collapsed on him as he slept in bed. Tragedy comes when we least expect it.

In 1988, Rebecca Schwab was elected Williamson County Superintendent of Schools (WCSS). She began her tenure with the responsibility of overseeing three new elementary schools that were just beginning to be built. A new school had not been built in Williamson County since 1976 when Fred J. Page High School was constructed on Arno Road. Mrs. Schwab, a longtime respected teacher, had no experience with construction, neither did anyone on her staff. She went to Mr. Ring for advice. His advice was, "Go talk to The Parent Company. They are building the new jail, and it is going well."

She did talk with us, and we were ultimately hired to oversee the three new schools. This led to a series of construction management contracts spanning more than a decade. From 1988 to 1999, The Parent Company managed the construction of eighteen new schools and nineteen facility additions and expansions for Williamson County School System.

The Parent Company set up offices in the Williamson County Administrative Complex with a staff that included Sharon Parsons, office manager; Becky Lawrence, clerk; Dan Cundiff, assistant project manager; and me, serving as project manager. There was a TPC superintendent on each school site while they were being constructed.

We did much more than manage the construction. I attended standing county commission building committee meetings with Mrs. Schwab to address construction questions. I helped her locate sites for new schools. A major responsibility was to work with the WCSS bookkeeper and attorney to manage the budget and legal agreements with the various cities and utilities

It wasn't long before A. C. Howell, budget director of Maury County, contacted us to see how we managed his neighboring county's projects. Maury officials had a bad experience with cost overruns on their school construction project. They were preparing to start two new schools and a new jail. I was happy to meet with Mr. Howell and, later, the full Maury County Board of Commissioners' Building Committee. We were awarded the management contract for the two schools and later the jail.

I enjoyed working with the Maury County Commission's Building Committee. The members were straight forward and unafraid to express their opinions. At the time, the Maury County Sheriff was at odds with the commissioners over the design of the new jail. The Sheriff went as far as hiring a jail consultant from Florida to attend a scheduled building committee meeting, at which time the consultant testified that the design of the new jail was wrong. Commissioners allowed him to speak. After he finished, no one spoke until one commissioner asked the consultant a question.

"Did you drive or fly from Florida?"

"I flew," the consultant answered.

The commissioner ended the conversation by saying, "Then you need to go to the Nashville airport, get on the plane going back to Florida, and tell the pilot not to fly over Maury County." The Sheriff and consultant left the meeting. No changes were made to the design.

In the late 1990's, commissioners recognized that the Maury County Courthouse, built in 1906, needed some major renovations. The courtrooms were outdated and the original cupola, one of its most notable architectural features, leaked. The Parent Company was hired to oversee the renovations.

The cupola, which stood 132 feet above street level, was examined by an engineer. His findings determined that the structure did not meet modern building codes for wind loads, i.e. the force of one strong tornado could blow it away. Because it was not feasible to repair it on site, Maury officials developed bid specifications and publicized the opportunity to construct a new cupola. The low bid was $500,000.

The existing cupola was removed and stored in a vacant lot nearby. The low bidder, Campbellsville Industries, salvaged some of the metal panels to use a template to duplicate the original cupola. Over a six-month-period a new cupola was fabricated in the Campbellsville, Kentucky plant. Individual pieces of the finished work were shipped to Columbia and assembled on the ground to form the new cupola. It was then lifted 132 feet and set on the Courthouse.

Every two years, I rode in a cage lifted by a crane and examined the cupola for chipping paint and cracks in the metal joints. This continued after I retired from The Parent Company. I made my last inspection in 2011.

The Crutcher family spent twelve good years at 121 Jefferson Drive in the Monticello subdivision of Franklin. Joyce was teaching high school math, first at Brentwood High School and then at Battle Ground Academy.

We made friends with a multitude of families: the Pitts, Tuckers, Drummers, McCormicks, Hagertys, Freemonts, and Hinemeyers to name a few. We all had children about the same age who grew up together. The annual trick-or-treat trek through the hundred home subdivision became a tradition. The fathers would "carry" the children through the neighborhood, while the mothers stayed at home and handed out the treats. Afterward, we would gather at someone's house for a community party.

Ray Tucker and I planted a garden on some vacant land adjacent to Jefferson Drive. We grew plenty of eggplant, tomatoes, okra and beans for our families and to share with our neighbors. I cleared the brush from land near the garden so that the children could have a small ball field. I was burning the brush when a wind arose. It blew the fire into the dry grass between the ball field and a field of plants that were being grown for landscaping. I had to call the fire department to extinguish the blaze. They stopped the fire before it got to the plants.

Elizabeth was our athlete. If a ball bounced, Elizabeth was there. Dan McCormick and I coached our daughters, Colleen and Elizabeth, in both basketball and softball when they were in elementary school. Susan was a cheerleader. When both girls attended BGA, we made almost all the games where they were playing or cheering.

I learned to keep my mouth shut when Elizabeth was playing in a game. I gave her and the coaches unsolicited advice, usually in a loud voice. This came to an end when Elizabeth said, "Dad, be quiet. I can listen to only one coach at a time." Dad shut up.

Part of Monticello was in the FEMA (Federal Emergency Management Agency) designated 100-year flood plain according to the official flood plain map. This map had been drawn with a two-foot error; it indicated the flood plain to extend farther into the lots than it actually did. I surveyed, as a licensed engineer, several of my neighbors lots to verify their houses were out of the flood plain. It was ironic that I had to hire and pay another engineer to survey and certify my house when we sold it.

We bought our present home in 1988. This house, located at 1324 Adams Street, is one block from our first house on Meadowlawn Drive. We had always admired it and wanted to buy it. But each time it sold, it was out of our reach. In 1988, a For Sale sign was placed in front of the house. I made an offer which was not accepted. Later, we saw a foreclosure notice in the newspaper stating that it would be sold on the steps of the Williamson County Courthouse. Joyce attended the auction on a stifling 100-degree day in July. She was the only bidder present. Her bid was not accepted because the bank had established a higher minimum bid. The auctioneer gave Joyce the bank's contact information. I followed up with the bank, Bank Boston. I was directed to speak to a lady in the division of distressed properties located in Florida.

Once I was able to talk with her and ask about the property, she nonchalantly said, "We are not ready to take offers. I will send an appraiser from Murfreesboro to look at the house. Call back in a week."

She called me four days later and asked, "What's your offer on the house? The appraiser said the roof is bad and we don't need to own this house with the winter coming. By the way, what happened to the swimming pool?"

I answered, "I understand the pool and a strip of land was sold by the previous owner to the developer of Adams Court for

$7,000. Adams Court is behind the house."

She seemed shocked and said, "We held the first lien on the house; the money from the sale should have gone to us. But that's not your problem. Make me an offer. We need to get this off our books." I offered her $20,000 less than I had offered the previous owner. She accepted. I had made a detailed inspection of the house so I knew what needed to be done. This included:

(1) a new roof,

(2) removal of three layers of wallpaper,

(3) new light fixtures,

(4) removal of carpet and refinishing of the hardwood floors,

(5) patching of plaster and new paint throughout.

I worked on Saturdays and Sunday afternoons doing what I could. We hired one man to strip the wallpaper. He steamed and scrapped wallpaper full time for three weeks.

Susan was reluctant to move from Monticello where many of her friends lived. That changed one winter afternoon when the Crutcher family was at the empty house. She went to the top of the 1900 staircase and walked down. "It would be fun coming down these stairs in my prom dress," she announced. Susan was a senior at BGA. This made her a little more excited about the move. She looked beautiful when she came down the stairs that spring on prom night.

We looked forward to moving back into our old neighborhood and across the street from our good friends, the Jim Roberts. Jim and Margaret had moved to Franklin from Memphis in 1977 and purchased an historic home on Adams Street. We had become close friends. Their sons were in BGA with our daughters, and we vacationed together in Destin, Florida.

Vacationing in those years created great memories. We went with the Hinemeyers and Hagertys to Seabrook Island, outside

Charleston, South Carolina. We spent one day just exploring the sites of Charleston, partially from atop a horse-drawn carriage we rented. Our horse was named Mike. At one point, Mike got spooked by the noise from a garbage truck and started running, pulling our carriage. Our driver was pulling on the reins frantically shouting, "Stop Mike, stop Mike!" We held on for a block before the driver got Mike under control.

We thought that the adventure was over until we looked behind us. Another horse drawn carriage was thundering toward us with, yes, you guessed it, another runaway horse. It had been spooked by Mike's escapade. This carriage's front wheels ran over our carriage's back wheels. A collision ensued and that carriage separated completely from its horse with the two front wheels heading toward the Battery and the Ashley River. Before anyone was thrown to their death, the back of the carriage stopped abruptly, dumping the driver and four ladies, all wearing sundresses, on the street. Luckily no one was injured.

We have since returned to Charleston with our daughter Elizabeth and her family. We took a carriage ride, but only after inquiring if the horse was the son of Mike. We were assured he was not.

The Crutcher family spent several summer vacations in Destin, Florida with the Roberts, the Dinard, and the Moody families. Jim Roberts' parents owned a condominium on the beach where they stayed. The Crutchers, Moodys and Dinards stayed in separate rentals nearby. Many nights, we gathered at the Roberts' condo to grill fish and enjoy the sunset. The children spent hours on the beach.

We set aside one day for deep sea fishing. The men and older children would arise before dawn, pick up donuts at the Donut Den, and then gather at the dock to board the charter fishing boat. Our captain would take us twenty-five miles out into the Gulf of Mexico where we would bottom fish until early afternoon. We caught the fish and the dock hands cleaned them for us. The cooking began once we got back to the Roberts' condo.

I was contacted by Woody Dinard around 1987 to talk about TPC building his new factory in Columbia, Tennessee. He had a small shop in Franklin fabricating industrial doors and told me he wanted to purchase land just outside Columbia where he could relocate the business. He had also purchased several long steel trusses that had been in a Dupont factory in New Johnsonville, Tennessee. TPC became the general contractor.

We hired Sessions Paving Company, headquartered in Nashville, to do the grading and paving. Sessions subcontracted the grading ('earth-moving') to a local company. I was the TPC principal-in-charge for this job, operating from my office in Brentwood. I received a call one morning from our foreman. He did not mince words. "You had better get down here. Our superintendent has threatened to kill the grading foreman!"

I made the 45-mile trip in record time. I confronted our superintendent.

"Did you threaten to kill the grading foreman?" I asked.

"Yes, I did, and I meant it," he said, recalling what happened. "We had a meeting in my trailer this morning with the architect. The Sessions foreman lied about something I said. After the

192

meeting, I caught the foreman outside and told him that if he told another lie about me, I would kill him. I also told him that if this had happened twenty years ago, when I was stronger, I would have gotten him in the trailer. But now I would need a 2x4. So, I told him, 'Don't turn your back on me!'"

As soon as I got back to Brentwood, I called the president of Sessions Paving and told him his contract with TPC required Sessions to have a full-time superintendent on site. They were to furnish one, and he was to relay messages between our superintendent and the grading foreman. They did, and we avoided a killing.

Shortly after this incident, an architect friend asked me if TPC had a job opening for his son. The son had started college but dropped out after one semester. I hired him to work as a laborer on the Columbia job. The young man did well and blended in with the rest of the crew.

After a few weeks, he went home and told his dad he was ready to go back to college. His father asked, "What prompted that decision?"

"I was eating Kentucky Fried Chicken at lunch today with another laborer. He was trying to figure out how he was going to scrape together enough money to get a new starter put on his old car. I realized that I need to learn to do something other than being a construction laborer. I am ready to get more education."

He did go back to college. He is now an architect.

The Parent Company's work in Williamson County continued beyond the jail project. At that time, the county's public recreation facilities and parks were organized and maintained by local volunteers. In 1989, the county commissioners decided to financially support a countywide recreation program by selling over $4 million worth of public bonds. This money was to be used to build a new recreation complex and upgrade the limited facilities throughout the county. In 1991, our company was selected to be the construction manager of this new program, which went well. The bulk of the work was the building of the recreation complex, which was to be built in the Judge Fulton Greer Park property, located off Hillsboro Road in Franklin. Additional bonds were sold, and more recreation buildings and parks were built in the county.

Susan graduated from Battle Ground Academy in 1989. This was the one hundredth anniversary of BGA's founding. The school planned an elaborate graduation ceremony in honor of the anniversary. Former Speaker of the United States House of Representatives Tip O'Neill was hired to be the graduation speaker. It was a hot day for May; the heat must have gotten to the Speaker. He referred to the school as Battle Creek Academy.

After eight years of teaching math at Brentwood High School, Joyce was recruited to teach at BGA. She joined the faculty and was able to teach until both daughters had graduated from college and were married. One downside for me was attending ballgames with her and being embarrassed by her enforcing the school's dress code. "Ol' Miss Crutcher" was what the students called her behind her back. But she did not hesitate to correct a student in front of the crowd. If they complained, she threatened to give them "time". In this case, "time" meant going to Saturday school or doing chores after school on weekdays. While this stern conversation was going on with an unfortunate student, I slid as far away from her as possible.

Susan went to Rhodes College in 1989 and had a good

194

experience there. She continued her studies at **Memphis State College** (now The University of **Memphis**). She received her **Master's** in Psychology, as well as her EdS in Psychology there. She presently practices in Virginia. Elizabeth decided to apply to Vanderbilt School of Engineering, my alma mater. This made for a proud daddy. She was accepted at Vanderbilt and enrolled in 1991. She received her Bachelor of Engineering degree in 1995. Later, she received her Professional Engineering license. After working in engineering and construction, Elizabeth is now a realtor with Dielmann Sotheby's International Realty in Saint Louis.

Susan was still living in **Memphis** when she met her future husband Andrew Chris Deneen. A recent graduate of **Milligan College**, he was teaching in **Memphis**. They were also active in local churches and Young Life.

Elizabeth had met her future husband, Charles Baxter Southern III, at Vanderbilt. They both graduated the same year. He has a degree from Vanderbilt's College of Arts and Sciences where his majors were computer science and political science. I have joked with Baxter that his double major qualified him to work with the CIA.

Our church, First Presbyterian Franklin, had outgrown the sanctuary and facility buildings in downtown Franklin. Land was purchased north of town on Franklin Road for a new church. I was active in the Church, and, in the effort to relocate, RFPs (Request for Proposals) were sent out to interested architectural and building firms. The Parent Company was selected to be the builder. During that process, I was serving on the building committee and offered to resign to avoid a conflict of interest. The committee asked me to stay on. One of my partners, Ti Bourland, became the principal-in-charge of what turned out to be a very successful project for both the church and The Parent Company.

We were able to build more than we originally anticipated with the funds available. The new sanctuary and accompanying facility was finished in 1994. I am proud to note that there was not the first conflict or disagreement; I was able to keep my church membership. The church added an educational wing in 1999, using The Parent Company. Presently, I serve on the church's task force overseeing the installation of a new organ. Again, The Parent Company is doing the general contracting work.

Susan and Chris married on July 22, 1995. Their evening wedding was the second in our new sanctuary. The reception was to be held in our backyard. Like all weddings, there was a little unexpected excitement. Earlier that day, a thunderstorm rolled into Franklin. We had been watching the weather forecast, so we knew the storm was coming. All the chairs and tables that had been set up on our lawn had to be moved under the tent that we had originally erected for the buffet table. Our neighbors—the Roberts, Davises, and Dinards—came to our rescue that afternoon before the pouring rains arrived. Thankfully, they all helped to move everything so we could focus on getting ready for the wedding ceremony.

After the storm passed, the chairs and tables had to be put back. Joyce and I could not stay to help since we had to get to the church early for wedding pictures. Again, we had help from our neighbors; Margaret Roberts and Lynn Davis brought ferns from their porches and made the serving area look lovely, and Baxter even came to help with the setup. Because he had been involved in all the moving and setting up on that hot day, Baxter needed to stay at our home to shower and get ready for the wedding. However, we had asked two ladies to stay at our house to watch over things while we were at the wedding ceremony. They did not know Baxter, so when he attempted to come inside to get ready, they refused to let him in the house. He finally convinced them that he was Elizabeth's boyfriend and needed to get ready for the wedding.

Joyce and I had booked a Caribbean cruise that began the week after the wedding. This was our first cruise and it turned out to be an adventure. A hurricane had developed out in the Gulf of Mexico and was headed toward Florida. The cruise ship shifted course and headed to Mexico to avoid the storm. We were due to stop at three ports, but because of the weather we could not stop at any. Our return route to Miami was changed as well. Instead, our capitan rerouted us south, giving us an unexpected trip that took our ship so close to Cuba that we could see land. We caught the tail end of the hurricane and spent one sleepless night being rolled in our bed. This was another time we were glad to get 'back to the good Ole USA'.

Baxter and Elizabeth were married on August 24, 1996, also at our church. The reception was held at Brentwood Country Club. We did not worry about the forecast that day since the reception was inside. One unique thing about the food served was the Key Lime Pie that Baxter wished to have rather than the traditional groom's cake. Joyce was a little hesitant about the pies, but there was not one single piece of pie to be found at the end of the night. Our guests loved his selection. What is most special to me though is that my 97-year-old grandmother, Mama Hicks, was able to attend both of our daughters' weddings. It's safe to say she enjoyed every minute.

197

15

HISTORIC MEETS MILLENNIAL

1998 – 2010

IN THE LATE 1990s, I was finishing the building of schools in Williamson County, as well as the new Maury County Jail. Williamson County's commissioners had just selected The Parent Company to be the construction manager for a new agriculture exhibit center. This facility was to contain a 150,000-square-foot exhibition hall and 100,000-square-foot assembly and office space. I was the principal-in-charge for TPC. We were hired at the same time the architect was selected, which meant we could be involved in the center's design. The design and construction took three years. The facility opened in May of 2001 with the annual Franklin Noon Rotary Club Rodeo as its debut event. This was a $14 million project.

Meanwhile, Williamson County had outgrown its courthouse, an iconic mid-nineteenth century building that anchors the Franklin Public Square. A new committee of commissioners was appointed to focus on the massive project. An architect was hired to design a new courthouse at a new location on Fourth Avenue South, just a block south of the existing building. The county commissioners set the budget at $9.2 million.

The Parent Company received the contract to be the construction manager at the same time the preliminary drawings were completed and presented. I was to be the principal-in-charge. Commissioners serving on the special Courthouse Building Committee were not happy with the design. The architects designed the building's exterior with a covering called EFIS 'External Insulation and Finishing Systems', which looks similar to stucco. The roof flashing was to be rubber membrane. The interior walls and ceilings were to be painted drywall, not plaster.

The committee chairman summarized the feelings of the committee when he said, "We want a building that looks a hundred years old and will last a hundred years. It must blend with the other old buildings in Franklin."

The architect's representative replied, "That can't be done with the budget you gave us."

"How much more will it cost to do what I outlined?" questioned the chairman.

"We don't know," was the representative's reply.

"Then get with The Parent Company and find out. We will meet in two weeks to receive the answer," directed the chairman.

Two weeks later, the committee met again. We told commissioners on the committee that the cost to upgrade would be an additional million dollars. They accepted the cost and got it approved by the full board of commissioners. The finished courthouse, now called the Williamson County Judicial Center, blends with the county's historic courthouse.

Foster and Creighton Company was a strong supporter of the Association of General Contractors 'AGC' at both the national and local levels. This commitment continued with The Parent Company. The AGC focuses on training and safety. All of TPC's partners were involved in the AGC, but I became the primary TPC representative. I attended and taught training classes and worked to get a strong safety program, including on-site safety inspections. I held various leadership positions including state president in 1999.

Due to my involvement with the AGC, Joyce and I attended the annual national conventions in cities across the country. We went to Washington, D.C., Honolulu, San Diego, Las Vegas, and Seattle. I also served on various national AGC committees and taskforces. The time I spent working with the AGC was very rewarding and time well spent.

My last major project with The Parent Company started with a knock on TPC's front door one morning before the start of the work day. The man at the door introduced himself as a member of Saint Ignatius Orthodox Church. He had been a kitchen equipment supplier to several of the schools built by The Parent Company. He told me he liked how we operated and had come to us to see if we were interested in building a new temple for Saint Ignatius. This was the only time an unsolicited job literally "walked through the front door."

The project was to build a new fellowship hall for the congregation, as well as to begin site work for a future temple and office spaces. This became one of my projects. It was a beautiful setting, situated down in the valley near Peytonsville. The priest, Father Stephen, and I became friends. He taught me about the Orthodox faith and how his church traces their origin back to the earliest Christians of ancient Antioch in the first century.

After I retired from TPC, I was hired by Saint Ignatius to be the owner's representative for their phase two expansion. The scope of this project was the building of a new temple, classrooms, offices, and the demolition of the existing temple.

In 2008, I retired from The Parent Company. A surprise luncheon was held with all of my family and many TPC workers present. Country music songwriter and artist Tom T. Hall even made an appearance and gave us a treasured performance of a few of his legendary songs. I was taken aback when he began singing a melody I had not heard before; it was written just for my retirement. Mr. Hall had been an acquaintance of Becky Lawrence, our office manager. I am grateful for his involvement and especially the gesture of kindness he showed to me and my family that day.

You can retire, but that does not always mean your work life is completely over. I did buy a fishing boat, but also agreed to complete two projects for TPC even though I had technically retired.

In early 2010, I was contacted by Wilson Staggs, a retired carpenter who had worked for TPC. He told me that he was tired of lying on the couch and wanted to know if I could help him find some small jobs in Franklin. He lived in Hohenwald, Tennessee, so his opportunities for projects were limited. I had been advising Joyce's cousin, Janice Swartz, on the construction of an addition to her house that included a garage. Janice was having problems with her builder. I took over the project work and hired Wilson and his brother Charles.

I had obtained a general contractor's license in 2008 as Crutcher and Associates LLC, so I was prepared to contract for small commercial and residential work. Wilson, Charles, and I worked for various clients until, due to health issues, the three of us retired a second time in 2017. Over our eight years together, we completed approximately one hundred jobs. We never had to advertise. Word of mouth got us all of the work we could handle.

There was another aspect of my career, one I began in 1984 and continues to this day. It is the role of being an expert witness in legal cases involving construction. It has been a very secondary part of my professional career, and yet I have been involved in forty-six cases. At the time of this writing, I am actively engaged in two cases. These usually involve an owner becoming dissatisfied with the work of a contractor or, in some cases, damage by a contractor to someone's property. Four of these cases involved loss of life.

My experience has also given me the opportunity to provide the service of cost certification for banks reviewing loans in the industry. I am hired to review draws from loans made to the contractors. I have provided this service to four banks over the years for approximately ten loans.

One of my greatest blessings is being involved with Joyce in the life of our church, First Presbyterian Franklin. We have been active ever since we joined on that Sunday in 1970. I have served as a deacon, elder, and Sunday school teacher. I have also served on a search committee for a pastor. These were all gratifying experiences, and in 2016 we were asked to co-chair, along with another couple, a capital campaign to retire the million-dollar mortgage on our church building. The result of this campaign was a $2 million commitment by our fellow members. The additional funds were used to renovate our 15-year-old facility. Today, I am honored to serve on the First Presbyterian Franklin's Preschool Committee. The church and the Christian faith are vital elements of my life.

Within the Franklin community, I have had the opportunity to work with several non-profit groups. The local Boys and Girls Club is a worthy organization that has grown from a start-up effort to a solid club that gives tremendous support to youth in Franklin and Fairview. I was asked to get involved in the 1990's when the idea of starting a local club first surfaced. In those days, the club met at what was an old office building on Columbia Pike near The Carter House, a property formerly used by the county's board of education. The property had originally been the site of the first Franklin High School, which was destroyed in a fire in the 1950s. The small office building the club was using was actually constructed in the 1960s after the high school was relocated to Hillsboro Road. An old gymnasium that had been salvaged from the school fire was also on the property. The idea was to use the office building for after-school programs for youth. The founding board for the club was able to hire a full-time director, Mr. Carter Savage. I am proud of the nearly three decades of work of The Boys and Girls Club in Williamson County.

Franklin Tomorrow is a group organized to bring Franklin together. I was asked to be one of the charter members in 1990. It is stronger than ever and continues to benefit Franklin.

In my opinion, affordable housing is a major need in Franklin and Nashville. I helped organize the Habitat for Humanity's branch for Franklin. Habitat has built over 250 houses in the counties of Williamson and Maury. It is quite humbling when you are recognized for your commitment. We have constructed twenty-six homes, all located in a single neighborhood near downtown Franklin. The membership surprised me in 2007 when they unveiled a new neighborhood entrance sign with these words etched in stone—The Ronald Crutcher Estates. The community can be accessed from Main Street, just before Carter's Creek Pike near the county's administrative complex, by turning right on Downs Boulevard, then turning right onto Good Neighbor Road and Helping Hands Drive.

Further opportunities to make a difference in affordable housing came when I was asked to become a board member of

The Housing Fund, which is based in Nashville. This organization finances affordable housing. Also, I was appointed to serve on the City of Franklin Housing Commission. My technical and broader professional experience has been helpful to various oversight committees within my community. I presently serve on the City of Franklin Building and Street Standards Board of Appeals; the Williamson County Board of Adjustments and Appeals; and the Williamson County Public Building Authority. Because I have been around Franklin and Williamson County so long, I tell people that my middle name has become "*Who do you know?*". I have been able to get to know our local government officials and local contractors. Knowing a lot of people can be positive in business and volunteerism.

16

UNEXPECTED DISCOVERIES

I AM GIVING A BRIEF medical history since it has been and remains the concern of my family and me. As previously written, I had always been very healthy but a persistent problem with my right kidney resulted in its removal in 1970. Unrelated, but worth noting, I was in Vietnam when the U.S. Forces were spraying defoliant, Agent Orange, to kill the vegetation along the roadways. Because of this the Veteran's Administration offers me full medical treatment. Some of my medical needs are met by the VA.

In the early eighties, I noticed that I could not hear the phone when it was on my left ear. I went to see Dr. Michael Mullins, a specialist who treats the ear, nose and throat, also known as an ENT. He examined me and took x-rays of my head. A few days later he had me come to his office. He had a serious look on his face.

"Have you ever been in a car accident or hit by a baseball bat?" was his opening remark.

"No. But when I was seven, I fell from an old cast iron stove and was knocked unconscious for a couple of minutes."

"Well, the x-rays show that part of your left brain is dead," he said.

"What does that mean?" I asked, quickly adding the obvious question. "Should I be concerned?"

Dr. Mullins said, "I asked Dr. Himmelfarb, the radiologist, the same questions. He said that if it had not caused problems, don't worry about it." I haven't worried about it, but I do use it as an excuse for not being able to learn a foreign language or play a musical instrument. I have worn hearing aids ever since.

My heart problems began about the same time as my hearing issue in the eighties. I felt some tightness in my chest, so I went to see my primary care physician, Dr. Richard Anderson. He diagnosed high blood pressure and prescribed a medicine for it. This was a disaster. The associated side effects of the drug were horrible; Dr. Anderson referred me to a high blood pressure specialist. This doctor prescribed a new medicine, which I took until 1996, when I almost passed out from a dizzy spell on the sidewalk in front of our house.

I went to Baptist Hospital and was diagnosed with possible blockages in my heart, which meant I needed an immediate non-invasive surgical procedure to determine if I needed stents, and, if so, to have them placed while I was on the operating table. This was Thanksgiving of 1996. The cardiologist was Dr. George Scoville; I met him for the first time in the operating waiting room at Baptist. We had plenty of time to get acquainted since the operating rooms were overbooked.

We discovered that both of us were BGA graduates and had had several of the same teachers. The procedure went well;

three stents were required. I was partially conscious and could watch him place the three stents. After a night in the hospital, I went home and had Thanksgiving dinner with the family.

Dr. Scovine became my cardiologist and remains so today. He had noticed that I had a heart murmur. By a series of tests, he determined that I had what is known as a "lazy valve". His diagnosis was to watch it to see if it continued to weaken. This was in 1997. I was thoroughly tested by various machines twice a year. Fasting was always required prior to the tests. I distinctly remember undergoing a treadmill stress test at Baptist Hospital. The room was on the fourth floor and overlooked a Krystal Restaurant. All I could think about while I was on the treadmill was the coffee and steamed Krystal burgers awaiting me after I finished my checkup. The Krystal is still there, and I make a point to stop for a meal whenever I am in the neighborhood.

Over the next few years, my heart continued to weaken. In 2006, Dr. Scovine gave me the bad news.

"Your lazy valve has laid down. You're going to have to have a new valve. You will need to decide whether you want an artificial valve or a pig valve," Dr. Scovine told me.

He went on to explain the difference. The artificial valve was made of stainless steel with a titanium flapper. It is expected to last a lifetime. It would require me to take blood thinner medication to keep blood clots from blocking the valve. The pig valve is taken from the carcass of a real pig. It would not require me to take blood thinner; however, it would last about twelve years. I was sixty-one years old and hoped to live more than twelve years. I chose the artificial valve. It is still ticking. When things are quiet you can hear a faint sound as it closes.

I try to follow all my doctors' instructions, particularly Dr. Scovine's. I question him often on medicines, procedures, etc. On one of my visits to his office, I had a list of questions and comments. I stopped and said, "I suppose I'm a hypochondriac."

His dry sense of humor kicked in and he replied, "You know what they put on the tombstone of a hypochondriac, don't you?"

"No," I answered.

"*I told you I was sick*," he answered with a chuckle.

I did not know it at the time of our vacation in 2015 to Key West, Florida, but there is a cemetery that has a gravestone with that very quote. If we vacation there again, I plan to visit that cemetery.

In 2012, I was in the midst of an arbitration hearing as an expert witness when I had an attack of gastric bleeding. I called my primary care doctor and arrangements were made to admit me to Williamson Medical Center (WMC). I was diagnosed with diverticulosis. This is when pockets called diverticula form in the walls of your digestive tract. The inner layer of your intestine pushes through weak spots in the outer lining. This pressure causes them to bulge out, making little pouches. The outer lining of my colon had become very thin. After a few days of treatment by manipulating my blood thinning medicine, I was discharged.

The next bleeding incident occurred in 2014. I had another attack and went straight to WMC's Emergency Room. Dr. Anderson, my primary care physician, had retired, and Dr. Sam Bastian was my new doctor. He organized a team to treat me, and they did. After the bleeding stopped and I had returned home, Dr. Bastian sent me to a surgeon in Nashville to examine me for potential surgery to remove part of my colon.

The surgeon, after reviewing my medical history and colon x-rays, told us he recommended against an operation. He was concerned about the effect of the anesthetic on my heart and valve.

My fourth episode with bleeding took place in 2016. Dr.

Bastian had instructed me to go to Saint Thomas Hospital's Emergency Room if I had another incident. Joyce carried me there early one morning; I was immediately admitted to the hospital's intensive care unit (ICU). After an examination, I was scheduled for surgery. The surgery involved the removal of over a foot of my colon. The recovery process was not easy. I was connected to a colostomy bag for six months.

After an inpatient hospital recovery period of about two weeks, I was strong enough to be transferred, by ambulance, to a skilled nursing facility, which was operated by National Healthcare Corporation (NHC) and located close to our home in the Cool Springs area of Franklin. I was extremely weak. I had physical therapy twice a day during my month-long stay at which time I returned home continuing my therapy several weeks through home health visits. During my stay at NHC that summer, my family came there and celebrated my birthday.

My latest incident occurred in 2019. I had a routine colonoscopy on June 20, 2019. Heavy bleeding started two days later, so once again Joyce rushed me to Saint Thomas. It was determined that a mix-up in the blood thinner medicine caused the bleeding. I was back in the ICU at Saint Thomas, a familiar place. While I was hooked up to IVs getting blood and glucose, my surgeon, Dr. Drew Reynolds, walked into my room. He normally had a smile on his face and was cheerful, but not this time. He had a full-size colorfully designed medical chart with him.

"I brought this chart to show you what I am going to remove, if I have to operate on you. It's the whole right side of your colon," he explained. The reality of my situation hit me. My prayers became a lot more frequent.

Joyce, as usual, was right there with me making sure I had everything I needed. Even before Dr. Reynolds had come into my room, she had quizzed another doctor with questions about potential procedures and post-operative care.

I remember one doctor politely asking her, "Are you a doctor? You seem to know all the terms."

"No, I'm a retired teacher. We have been through this before, many times." Joyce answered.

Thanks to some excellent doctors, nurses, and answered prayers, my bleeding stopped. I was able to go home ten days later, June 30, but only for one night. I got so weak that I couldn't get out of bed. On July 1, Joyce called an ambulance. The attendants got me into it, strapped me down, and started an IV. Back to the ICU and more tests. This time the problem was my gallbladder and gallstones. The gallstones were blocking the bile duct. Since I was taking the blood thinner Coumadin, I could not have the operation immediately. I had to undergo a drug treatment of heparin medication for a few days. In the meantime, a stent was placed in my bile duct to keep it open. On July 5, I had my gall bladder removed.

After a week at Saint Thomas, I went back to NHC for therapy. But during my hospital stay, I was able to watch every game of the Vanderbilt baseball team's march to the 2019 National Collegiate Athletic Association's Championship. While at NHC some good friends came by to visit and brought me a Vanderbilt University Championship commemorative shirt. My Saint Louis Crutcher clan sent me a championship hat the next day by FedEx.

Presently, I am relatively healthy for someone seventy-five years old. I have an artificial heart valve, pacemaker, hearing aids, orthopedic shoes, and glasses. I am old and hope to get older. As I said in the preface to this book, I have undertaken this project primarily for my five grandchildren. Since our first grandson Andrew was born in 2000 until now, my greatest pleasure and enjoyment is spending time with them, their parents and Joyce.

Our first outing with a grandchild, an only grandchild at

that time, was with Andrew and his parents, Chris and Susan. We went to Topsail Beach and watched baby Andrew play with his animal mobile. This was the beginning of years of family vacations to come.

The announcement of the upcoming birth of our second grandchild, Charlie B., was unusual. Our son-in-law, Baxter, was sent to London, England for a four-month training program at Lloyd's of London. Elizabeth accompanied him. They invited us to come visit, and we did. After a daylong transcontinental flight, we arrived at their flat at 2:00 a.m. expecting to be quietly greeted before turning in for the "night" to finally go to bed. To our surprise, we were greeted instead by a small snack tray, refreshments, and a photograph. After staring a few minutes at the black and white photo, I asked, "What's this?"

"Your new grandson," answered a smiling Elizabeth. It was an ultra-sound image of Charles Baxter Southern IV. I was able to tell that he was a boy.

While in London, Elizabeth became the ultimate travel guide while Baxter went to his training class. She took us to Buckingham Palace, several museums, and other special places in London. We even went under the English Channel in the Chunnel train for an overnight trip to Paris. Coming into Paris our train was delayed outside the terminal yard. After about thirty minutes the conductor said that an unclaimed backpack had been left on the station's loading platform. The French security blew it up, and we were then allowed to debark. This was in 2000, before 9/11.

We spent the night and the next day sightseeing. We saw the Louvre Museum, the Eiffel Tower, and the place of Princess Diana's fatal automobile crash in 1997. We rested on the train as we returned to London. One day while Joyce and Elizabeth shopped, Baxter gave me a tour of Lloyd's

213

of London. I remember seeing the bell that is rung every time a ship is lost. After a great tour, Baxter carried me to the local neighborhood pub, The Elephant and Castle.

In 2011, the Crutcher clan descended upon Disney World in Orlando. By this time, we had our full complement of five grandchildren, Elizabeth ('4), Mac ('8), Ellen Anne ('8), Charlie B. ('10), and Andrew ('11). We stayed in the Polynesian Village and made numerous treks to the Disney park. We had a blast! Dinner in Cinderella's Castle, the Halloween parade, and the rides are just a few of the many things we enjoyed. I still hear the voices of "It's A Small World" playing over again in my head.

We celebrated our fiftieth wedding anniversary August 12, 2017. Joyce and I marked the occasion by gathering the Crutcher clan in New York City for a week-long trip the first week of July. All eleven of us had a fantastic time together. Our hotel was located just off Broadway and Times Square and overlooked the Theater District. The older grandchildren were of the age that they could explore on their own. The first night, we all went to a restaurant and dined on the outdoor patio overlooking Bryant Park. As we were being served a thunderstorm came, and we finished our meal under umbrellas. We walked to see a performance of *The Lion King* and to take in the majestic views of the Fourth of July fireworks display along the Hudson River.

The trip to the Statue of Liberty via the World Trade Center Memorial was another group outing. The WTC Memorial was a sobering experience as we stopped to reflect on September 11, 2001. Another day, we split up so that some of us could visit our friend Jeff Moody, who worked for MLS Baseball. He gave us a tour of their operations, including the bullpen where all the Major League games are monitored. Because of security, we had to be out of that part of the building before the one o'clock game began. We had lunch with Jeff at a local pizza joint. That was some delicious pizza.

Our daughters and sons-in-law treated us to an elaborate anniversary dinner at a nice restaurant in the Theater District. After a memorable, fun-filled week we flew back to our respective hometowns in Lynchburg, Virginia; Saint Louis, Missouri; and Nashville.

17

CONSIDERATIONS — PAST, PRESENT AND FUTURE

AS I COMPLETE THIS BOOK, there are several thoughts that continue to run through my mind about various topics. I will share them as they come to me; they are in no particular order.

With time and age, I realize just how much I appreciate my military service. I went into the Army through the ROTC program, and, truthfully, I got into ROTC to meet my Vandy physical education requirement, plus the fifty dollars a month payment I received for the last two years of college. Our country was at the beginning of the heavy US commitment to South Vietnam. The draft was being used, but I avoided it by being in ROTC. I served my time, was discharged, and came home. Slowly, I came to appreciate those who didn't make it home, those who had it rougher than I. There are ten names recorded on the commemorative plaque mounted on the façade of the

217

Williamson County archives building honoring the Vietnam soldiers from communities throughout our county who died in the Vietnam war. I knew four of them.

I have an uncle who served in World War II; another, now deceased, who served in the Korean War; and a first cousin, who served with me in Vietnam. For several years, the four of us would gather and spend two or three hours reminiscing. No one else was around. That was a good thing because three of us had hearing aids and tended to talk loudly. We finished the day by going to O'Charley's Restaurant for their free Veteran's Day meal. It was time well spent.

I am pleased that the public makes it a priority to thank veterans for their service. This is a major turnaround from the decades after the Vietnam War. Recently, with the aid of State Representative Glen Casada and Williamson County Mayor Rogers Anderson, I helped the family of Richard Carothers get a local bridge memorialized for his service. Richard was killed in Vietnam in 1966. At one time, he and I worked together in the tobacco fields of our county. Richard Carothers was a good person.

I have fond memories of times spent with grandchildren, their parents, and their other grandparents. We visited with the elder Deneens, Mariane and Fred, at their mountain lodge in Spruce Pine, North Carolina. Many happy weekends were spent with the elder Southerns, Jana and Charlie, at their lake home on Kentucky Lake. Often Jana's mother, Deema Atterbury, "Mama D," would be with them. No trip there would be complete without a catfish dinner at the Catfish Kitchen.

I continue to be active in my church, First Presbyterian Franklin, with its various groups, like Sunday school and the Growth Group—all are guiding me to a better understanding of the Christian faith. One might say I am cramming for the final exam. I am ready to die, but am in no hurry!

218

Do I regret not doing something in the past? Yes, not learning to play golf. I had three TPC partners who played, so I decided they could conduct the "golf course business" and I would do other things. I played one round with my minister, Tim Croft, and a church friend. I enjoyed every minute of it. It would have been a good hobby in my retirement. Other than that, no, I have no regrets. I have always "rolled with the punches" and there haven't been many.

I plan to remain active in the various organizations to which I belong. The first of these is the Rotary Club of Franklin at Breakfast. My tenure goes back to 1990 when twenty members chartered this club. I have gone with members to Guatemala to see how we could help the people have a better life. We determined they need clean, safe water. We are presently working with the USPCA Church to install small water treatment units in the village schools. Locally, we focus on education and feeding the hungry.

My work with Habitat for Humanity does and will continue. I have previously described my past involvement. I am currently working to get a house built for another desiring future homeowner. Most of my volunteer efforts are for The Housing Fund. The opportunities continue to arise to help develop relationships with local banks and borrowers. The Legacy Board of Franklin Tomorrow, composed of retired members, will occupy some of my time. Franklin Tomorrow is an organization that promotes Franklin by bringing the community together with informational programs and gatherings.

Of course, I must set aside time in my future for doctors. One of my favorite sayings is, "If it weren't for doctors, I would have no social life at all!" A highlight occurred recently when my GI doctor scheduled another procedure in five years when I will be eighty.

The future? I am looking forward to more time with Joyce, Susan, Elizabeth, Chris, Baxter, Andrew, Charlie B., Ellen Anne, Mac, and Elizabeth. What does the future hold? I don't know, but I am looking forward to it.

I was working for Foster and Creighton Company when they served as the general contractor for the mammoth Vanderbilt Stadium renovation project.

Vanderbilt's Dudley Field, ca. 1980, was established in 1923 and named in memory of Dr. William Dudley, the first dean of the medical school and founding supporter of the Southeastern Intercollegiate Athletic Association.

One major impact of the project was seen in the size and conveniences offered in the new press box and VIP area as compared to the original, shown above.

Every stage of the Stadium expansion required coordination with many subcontractors.

The Stadium was completed as promised by the 1981 football season opener against the University of Maryland. Vanderbilt was victorious on September 12, 1981.

Dudley Field Work On Schedule

By MIKE MORROW

● Photo on Page 69

Like a coaching staff in the midst of a hectic fourth quarter rally, overseers of the new Vanderbilt football stadium construction are being kept busy these days.

Workers at the site, where the old 34,000-seat structure is being replaced by a spanking new 44,000-seat facility, are still on schedule and fully expect to have the stadium ready for Vandy's season opener against Maryland Sept. 12.

IT'S STILL a busy schedule for Dudley Field workers. And, according to officials with the construction crew and Vandy athletic offices, the schedule is a tight one at that.

"A lot has to happen, and a lot is happening," Ron Crutcher,

project manager at the site, said yesterday. "It's been very hectic around here lately."

The final sections of precast concrete are to be added to the structure next week, while portions of the pre-cast concrete to be set, about 1,250 have been put in place, Crutcher said.

MOST OF the major portions of the project have been accomplished, although there is still work to be done on such areas as rest rooms, concession stands and some press box duties. Seats around the stadium are currently being put into place. Installation of the field's artificial turf is scheduled to begin Aug. 1, Crutcher said.

Vanderbilt athletic director Roy Kramer said the schedule is demanding, and he is optimistic about the September unveiling.

"It is a tight schedule," said Kramer. "We're staying with it. It is significant when you're talking about building a totally new structure within a limited space of time."

CONSTRUCTION ON the new stadium began almost immediately after the completion of last year's football season.

"It's not like an office building where you can occupy half of it while you're finishing the other half," said Crutcher, working for the Foster & Creighton construction firm handling the project. "You've got to have a lot of things done."

Crutcher said setbacks in the construction schedule have been

few, noting the recent rain as one deterrent. "It seemed like the rain we had lately hurt us as much as the weather all winter. It seemed it rained every other day, and always at the stadium. "There have been no problems out of the ordinary, though."

The Tennessean covered our progress with much anticipation in 1980 and 1981.

Up in the Air Over Stadium Repair

The bleachers at Vanderbilt University's Dudley Field look like they are suspended from the clouds after being lifted yesterday to reinforce the steel and allow for the addition of more than 6,000 seats. The expansion is scheduled to be completed before the next football season. Story on Page 21.

This Tennessean coverage captured the precision involved in raising the bleachers so that precast concrete could be installed.

227

SAM DAVIS HOTEL — 7TH AVE. AT COMMERCE — NASHVILLE, TENN.

250 ROOMS EACH WITH TUB AND SHOWER BATHS
AND CIRCULATING ICE WATER

5A-H609

The new Nashville Convention Center required the demolition of the iconic Sam Davis Hotel, established in 1927. (Courtesy Nashville Metro archives)

The Parent Company oversaw the implosion in 198s. Notice the Sam Davis Hotel sign falling, right of the building. (Courtesy Nashville Metro Archives)

The Parent Company hosted a gathering for officials and business executives to view the implosion from atop another iconic Nashville building, the National Life and Casualty Insurance Company. (Courtesy Nashville Metro Archives)

Clouds of smoke and debris filled the downtown streets, while curious onlookers watched from safe distances. (Courtesy Nashville Metro Archives)

In 1984, I was asked to join a team of colleagues formerly of Foster and Creighton to establish a new construction firm in Brentwood.

MIDDLE TENNESSEE BRANCH

I maintained an active membership in the AGCA for many years during my professional career, serving in leadership and educational roles as needed.

The Nashville Convention Center became a beacon to the downtown Nashville district in the eighties. (Courtesy of The Parent Company)

The interior of the Nashville Convention Center, which accommodated numerous events and expositions, was a vital economic development tool as the region grew. It has been replaced by the Music City Convention Center.

Working with my church, First Presbyterian Church Franklin, on this new sanctuary was a highlight of my career. (Courtesy The Parent Company)

The Williamson County Agricultural Exposition Center, ca. 2003, is an important part of the culture of my community. (Courtesy of the Parent Company)

Overseeing the construction management for a new Williamson County Courthouse, just a block from the original antebellum courthouse of 1858 was a historic project for our firm and the community. (Courtesy of The Parent Company)

Saint Ignatius Orthodox Church is situated in a pastoral hamlet of Williamson County near the community of Peytonsville. (Courtesy The Parent Company)

The interior of this house of worship is especially breathtaking. Working on Saint Ignatious gave me much satisfaction. (Courtesy The Parent Company)

Elizabeth, standing, Joyce, Susan and I, ca. 1987.

Joyce and I in London in 2004.

Joyce taught Geometry, algebra I, and algebra II for many years in Williamson County schools and at my alma mater, Battle Ground Academy. Her years teaching at BGA are some of her most treasured.

Baxter Southern, left, and Chris Deneen have been great additions to our family and wonderful husbands to our daughters Elizabeth, left, and Susan.

236

These three photos have something in common that Joyce and I are very proud to share: the love of marriage, the love of family, and the celebration of great baking. The Deneens, left, and Southerns followed our lead with the cake.

237

Our trip to Disney with our grandchildren, from left, Andrew Deneen, Ellen Anne Deneen, Charlie B. Southern IV, Elizabeth Deneen, and Mac Southern.

Our grandchildren Elizabeth and Ellen Anne, seated, with Mac, standing left, Charlie B. and Andrew at a family gathering in Saint Louis 2018.

ABOUT THE AUTHOR

A Williamson County, Tennessee native, Ronald Crutcher is retired from The Parent Company, a construction management firm he helped found in 1984. He was formerly with Foster and Creighton Company, a 100-year-old Nashville-based construction concern, where he helped lead the first major renovation and expansion of Vanderbilt Stadium since its establishment in 1923. He played a major role in the construction of The First American Center in downtown Nashville, at which time a prehistoric cave was discovered during excavation. The relics unearthed in 1971 were secured by archaeologists and later became the inspiration for naming Nashville's hockey team, The Predators. His assignment to oversee the expansion of the King Faisal Specialist Hospital in Riyadh, Saudi Arabia was his second experience overseas and one that solidified his love of the "good ole USA."

Beginning in the eighties, he managed the construction of nearly two dozen schools and, in 2004, the new Williamson County Courthouse. A graduate of Battle Ground Academy and Vanderbilt University School of Engineering, he is a Vietnam veteran who served with the 35th Engineer Group of the U.S. Army. He has volunteered his time and talents to support such non-profits as Habitat for Humanity; The Housing Fund; The Franklin Rotary at Breakfast; the Boys and Girls Club; and Franklin Tomorrow. He and his wife Joyce reside in Franklin, where they attend Franklin First Presbyterian Church. The couple's two adult daughters reside in Missouri and Virginia with their families.